Series/Number 07-136

MISSING DATA

PAUL D. ALLISON
University of Pennsylvania

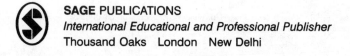

SAGE PUBLICATIONS
International Educational and Professional Publisher
Thousand Oaks   London   New Delhi

For information:

Sage Publications, Inc.
2455 Teller Road
Thousand Oaks, California 91320
E-mail: order@sagepub.com

Sage Publications Ltd.
6 Bonhill Street
London EC2A 4PU
United Kingdom

Sage Publications India Pvt. Ltd.
M-32 Market
Greater Kailash I
New Delhi 110 048 India

Printed in the United States of America

Library of Congress Cataloging-in-Publication Data

Allison, Paul David.
    Missing data / by Paul D. Allison.
        p.   cm. – (Quantitative applications in the social sciences
    (Qass) ; no. 07-136)
    Includes bibliographical references and index.
    ISBN 978-0-7619-1672-7 (p)
        1. Mathematical statistics. 2. Missing observations (Statistics)
    I. Title.   II. Series: Sage university papers series.   Quantitative applications in
the social sciences; no. 07-136
    QA276 .A55   2001
    001.4'22–dc21   2001001295

This book is printed on acid-free paper.

07   10   9   8   7

Acquiring Editor:	C. Deborah Laughton
Editorial Assistant:	Eileen Carr
Production Editor:	Denise Santoyo
Production Assistant:	Kathryn Journey
Typesetter:	Technical Typesetting Inc.

When citing a university paper, please use the proper form. Remember to cite the Sage University Paper series title and include paper number. One of the following formats can be adapted (depending on the style manual used):

(1) ALLISON, P. D. (2001) *Missing Data.* Sage University Papers Series on Quantitative Applications in the Social Sciences, 07-136. Thousand Oaks, CA: Sage.

OR

(2) Allison, P. D. (2001). *Missing Data.* (Sage University Papers Series on Quantitative Applications in the Social Sciences, series no. 07-136). Thousand Oaks, CA: Sage.

CONTENTS

SERIES EDITOR'S INTRODUCTION

Problems of missing data are pervasive in empirical social science research. The statistical results reported with most nonexperimental studies rest on sample sizes smaller, sometimes much smaller, than the initial number of selected cases. A relatively few absent observations on a handful of variables can quickly reduce the effective N. With an opinion survey for example, it is not uncommon for a multivariate analysis to halve the original draw. Suppose Professor Mary Rose, of the Business School, is examining a probability sample of $N = 1,000$ respondents, in a survey of consumer attitudes and behavior. She estimates a reasonably specified multiple regression model of spending, employing the usual computer option of *listwise deletion* (i.e., any respondent with data lacking on any model variable is excluded). As a result, the actual cases available fall to $N = 499$. Serious questions arise. Do these 499 still "represent" the population? Are the coefficients possessing of any desirable properties? Is the sample too small for rejection of null hypotheses? In order to keep sample size, should pairwise deletion have been tried? Or, are there altogether new approaches worth considering? These questions, and others, are addressed in this splendid monograph by Paul Allison.

"Observations are randomly missing." That is the stock argument for going ahead in the face of data attrition, relying on the cases left. But the assumption is vague, and may not be saving. Suppose the observations are "missing completely at random" (labeled MCAR by Allison)? That means that none of the variables, dependent (Y) or independent (X), has missing scores related to the values of the variable itself. For example, with the spending variable above, nonresponse should be no more likely for big spenders than small spenders. Given the same condition held for the other model variables, then the subsample of 499 would represent a scientific draw, permitting valid inferences. In particular, it allows the regression estimates to be unbiased and consistent. This variety of randomness, MCAR, is the problem-free sort researchers may like to claim, but it makes very strong assumptions.

Somewhat more realistic is the assumption that observations are "missing at random" (MAR). Here missing data on a variable, say Y, are held to be random if, after controlling for other variables, the value of Y cannot predict the location of the missing scores. So in the foregoing illustration, occupational status (X) might be correlated with missing data on spending, with high-status respondents more likely to underreport spending. Once X is on the right-hand side, missing observations on Y behave randomly. Under the condition of MAR, the missing data-generating mechanism is *ignorable*, as Allison puts it. The focus of his monograph is on methods for dealing with improved estimation under the MAR condition, although he does address the difficult circumstance of *nonignorable* missing data mechanisms.

If the data are MAR, then the quality of estimation rests heavily on the location of the systematic error. Encouragingly, when missing data correlations are confined to the independent variables, then listwise deletion can still yield unbiased estimates. For instance, in the example, missing data on occupational status, X, might be related to missing data on another independent variable, age (Z); e.g., those not reporting age might be older and of higher status. Given that older age does not relate to the reporting of spending, then no bias is expected. Indeed, as Allison so artfully demonstrates, under a range of MAR conditions, the standard listwise deletion option can outperform the traditional missing data correction methods of pairwise deletion, dummy variable adjustment, or mean substitution.

New approaches to handling missing data problems take up the bulk of the monograph. After a review of maximum likelihood (ML) estimation given missing data, he explicates the EM algorithm for imputation, with a carefully selected data example on graduation rates in American colleges. The final chapters go beyond the ML approach, in an explication of multiple imputation (MI) methods, and a discussion of nonignorable missing data. The work presents a tour de force of the latest techniques for handling missing data, a topic poorly developed in almost all stat books. Paul Allison also wisely reminds us that the best solution to the missing data problem "is not to have any." But if you have it and seek a remedy, this is the book to buy.

—*Michael S. Lewis-Beck*
Series Editor

MISSING DATA

PAUL D. ALLISON
University of Pennsylvania

1. INTRODUCTION

Sooner or later (usually sooner), anyone who does statistical analysis runs into problems with missing data. In a typical data set, information is missing for some variables for some cases. In surveys that ask people to report their income, for example, a sizable fraction of the respondents typically refuse to answer. Outright refusals are only one cause of missing data. In self-administered surveys, people often overlook or forget to answer some of the questions. Even trained interviewers occasionally may neglect to ask some questions. Sometimes respondents say that they just do not know the answer or do not have the information available to them. Sometimes the question is inapplicable to some respondents, such as asking unmarried people to rate the quality of their marriage. In longitudinal studies, people who are interviewed in one wave may die or move away before the next wave. When data are collated from multiple administrative records, some records may have become inadvertently lost.

For all these reasons and many others, missing data are a ubiquitous problem in both the social and health sciences. Why is it a problem? Because nearly all standard statistical methods presume that every case has information on all the variables to be included in the analysis. Indeed, the vast majority of statistical textbooks have nothing whatsoever to say about missing data or how to deal with it.

There is one simple solution that everyone knows and that is usually the default for statistical packages: If a case has any missing data for any of the variables in the analysis, then simply exclude that case from the analysis. The result is a data set that has no missing data and can be analyzed by any conventional method. This strategy is commonly known in the social sciences as *listwise deletion* or *casewise deletion*, but also goes by the name of *complete case analysis*.

In addition to its simplicity, listwise deletion has some attractive statistical properties, which will be discussed later. It also has a major

1

disadvantage that is apparent to anyone who has used it: In many applications, listwise deletion can exclude a large fraction of the original sample. For example, suppose you have collected data on a sample of 1,000 people and you want to estimate a multiple regression model with 20 variables. Each of the variables has missing data on 5% of the cases, and the chance that data are missing for one variable is independent of the chance that it is missing on any other variable. You could then expect to have complete data for only about 360 of the cases, discarding the other 640. If you merely downloaded the data from a web site, you might not feel too bad about this, although you might wish you had a few more cases. On the other hand, if you had spent $200 per interview for each of the 1,000 people, you might have serious regrets about the $130,000 that was wasted (at least for this analysis). Surely there must be some way to salvage something from the 640 incomplete cases, many of which may lack data on only one of the 20 variables.

Many alternative methods have been proposed, and several of them will be reviewed in this book. Unfortunately, most of these methods have little value, and many of them are inferior to listwise deletion. That's the bad news. The good news is that statisticians have developed two novel approaches to handling missing data—maximum likelihood and multiple imputation—that offer substantial improvements over listwise deletion. Although the theory behind these methods has been known for at least a decade, it is only in the last few years that they have become computationally practical. Even now, multiple imputation or maximum likelihood can demand a substantial investment of time and energy, both in learning the methods and in carrying them out on a routine basis. But, if you want to do things right, you usually have to pay a price.

Both maximum likelihood and multiple imputation have statistical properties that are about as good as we can reasonably hope to achieve. Nevertheless, it is essential to keep in mind that these methods, like all the others, depend on certain easily violated assumptions for their validity. Not only that, there is no way to test whether or not the most crucial assumptions are satisfied. The upshot is that although some missing data methods are clearly better than others, none of them really can be described as good. The only really good solution to the missing data problem is not to have any. So in the design and execution of research projects, it is essential to put great effort into minimizing the occurrence of missing data. Statistical adjustments can never make up for sloppy research.

2. ASSUMPTIONS

Researchers often try to make the case that people who have missing values on a particular variable are no different from those with observed measurements. It is common, for example, to present evidence that people who do and do not report their income are not significantly different on a variety of other variables. More generally, researchers have often claimed or assumed that their data are "missing at random" without a clear understanding of what that means. Even statisticians were once vague or equivocal about this notion. However, Rubin (1976) put things on a solid foundation by rigorously defining different assumptions that might plausibly be made about missing data mechanisms. Although his definitions are rather technical, I will try to convey an informal understanding of what they mean.

Missing Completely at Random

Suppose there are missing data on a particular variable Y. The data on Y are said to be *missing completely at random* (MCAR) if the probability of missing data on Y is unrelated to the value of Y itself or to the values of any other variables in the data set. When this assumption is satisfied for all variables, the set of individuals with complete data can be regarded as a simple random subsample from the original set of observations. Note that MCAR does allow for the possibility that "missingness" on Y is related to "missingness" on some other variable X. For example, even if people who refuse to report their age invariably refuse to report their income, it is still possible that the data could be missing completely at random.

The MCAR assumption *would be* violated if people who did not report their income were younger, on average, than people who did report their income. It would be easy to test this implication by dividing the sample into those who did and did not report their income, and then testing for a difference in mean age. If there are, in fact, no systematic differences on the fully observed variables between those with data present and those with missing data, then the data are said to be *observed at random*. On the other hand, just because the data pass this test does not mean that the MCAR assumption is satisfied. Still there must be no relationship between missingness on a particular variable and the values of that variable.

Although MCAR is a rather strong assumption, there are times when it is reasonable, especially when data are missing as part of the research design. Such designs are often attractive when a particular variable is very expensive to measure. The strategy then is to measure the expensive variable only for a random subset of the larger sample, implying that data are missing completely at random for the remainder of the sample.

Missing at Random

A considerably weaker assumption is that the data are *missing at random* (MAR). Data on Y are said to be missing at random if the probability of missing data on Y is unrelated to the value of Y, after controlling for other variables in the analysis. To express this more formally, suppose there are only two variables X and Y, where X always is observed and Y sometimes is missing. MAR means that

$$\Pr(Y\text{missing}|Y, X) = \Pr(Y\text{missing}|X).$$

In words, this expression means that the conditional probability of missing data on Y, given both Y and X, is equal to the probability of missing data on Y given X alone. For example, the MAR assumption would be satisfied if the probability of missing data on income depended on a person's marital status, but within each marital status category, the probability of missing income was unrelated to income. In general, data are *not* missing at random if those individuals with missing data on a particular variable tend to have lower (or higher) values on that variable than those with data present, controlling for other observed variables.

It is impossible to test whether the MAR condition is satisfied, and the reason should be intuitively clear. Because we do not know the values of the missing data, we can not compare the values of those with and without missing data to see if they differ systematically on that variable.

Ignorable

The missing data mechanism is said to be ignorable if (a) the data are MAR and (b) the parameters that govern the missing data process are unrelated to the parameters to be estimated. Ignorability basically means that there is no need to model the missing data mechanism as part of the estimation process. However, special techniques certainly are needed to utilize the data in an efficient manner. Because it is hard to imagine real-world applications where condition (b) is not satisfied, I treat MAR and ignorability as equivalent conditions in this book. Even in the rare situation where condition (b) is not satisfied, methods that assume ignorability work just fine, but you could do even better by modeling the missing data mechanism.

Nonignorable

If the data are not MAR, we say that the missing data mechanism is nonignorable. In that case, usually the missing data mechanism must be modeled to get good estimates of the parameters of interest. One widely used method for nonignorable missing data is Heckman's (1976) two-stage estimator for regression models with selection bias on the dependent variable. Unfortunately, for effective estimation with nonignorable missing data, *very* good prior knowledge about the nature of the missing data process usually is needed, because the data contain no information about what models would be appropriate and the results typically will be very sensitive to the choice of model. For these reasons and because models for nonignorable missing data typically must be quite specialized for each application, this book puts the major emphasis on methods for ignorable missing data. In the last chapter, I briefly survey some approaches to handling nonignorable missing data. In Chapter 3, we will see that listwise deletion has some very attractive properties with respect to certain kinds of nonignorable missing data will be evident.

3. CONVENTIONAL METHODS

Although many different methods have been proposed for handling missing data, only a few have gained widespread popularity. Unfortunately, none of the widely used methods is clearly superior to listwise deletion. In this section, I briefly review some of these methods, starting with the simplest. In evaluating these methods, I will be particularly concerned with their performance in regression analysis (including logistic regression and Cox regression), but many of the comments also apply to other types of analysis as well.

Listwise Deletion

As already noted, listwise deletion is accomplished by deleting from the sample any observations that have missing data on any variables in the model of interest and then applying conventional methods of analysis for complete data sets. There are two obvious advantages to listwise deletion: (1) it can be used for any kind of statistical analysis, from structural equation modeling to log-linear analysis; (2) no special computational methods are required. Depending on the missing data mechanism, listwise deletion also can have some attractive statistical properties. Specifically, if the data are MCAR, then the reduced sample will be a random subsample of the original sample. This implies that, for any parameter of interest, if the estimates would be unbiased for the full data set (with no missing data), they also will be unbiased for the listwise deleted data set. Furthermore, the standard errors and test statistics obtained with the listwise deleted data set will be just as appropriate as they would have been in the full data set.

Of course, the standard errors generally will be larger in the listwise deleted data set because less information is utilized. They also will tend to be larger than standard errors obtained from the optimal methods described later in this book, but at least you do not have to worry about making inferential errors because of the missing data—a big problem with most of the other commonly used methods.

On the other hand, if the data are not MCAR, but only MAR, listwise deletion can yield biased estimates. For example, if the probability of missing data on schooling depends on occupational status, regression of occupational status on schooling will produce a biased estimate of the regression coefficient. So, in general, it appears that listwise deletion is not robust to violations of the MCAR assumption. Surprisingly, however, listwise deletion is the method that is *most* robust to violations of MAR among *independent* variables in a regression analysis. Specifically, if the probability of missing data on any of the independent variables does *not* depend on the values of the *dependent* variable, then regression estimates using listwise deletion will be unbiased (if all the usual assumptions of the regression model are satisfied).[1]

For example, suppose that we want to estimate a regression model to predict annual savings. One of the independent variables is income, for which 40% of the data are missing. Suppose further that the probability of missing data on income is highly dependent on both income and years of schooling, another independent variable in the model. As long as the probability of missing income does not depend on *savings*, the regression estimates will be unbiased (Little, 1992).

Why is this the case? Here is the essential idea. It is well-known that disproportionate stratified sampling on the independent variables in a regression model does not bias coefficient estimates. A missing data mechanism that depends only on the values of the independent variables is essentially equivalent to stratified sampling, that is, cases are being selected into the sample with a probability that depends on the values of those variables. This conclusion applies not only to linear regression models, but also to logistic regression, Cox regression, Poisson regression, and so on.

In fact, for logistic regression, listwise deletion gives valid inferences under even broader conditions. If the probability of missing data on any variable depends on the value of the dependent variable but does *not* depend on any of the independent variables, then logistic regression with listwise deletion yields consistent estimates of the slope coefficients and their standard errors (Vach, 1994). The intercept estimate will be biased, however. Logistic regression with listwise deletion is problematic only when the probability of any missing data depends on *both* the dependent and independent variables.[2]

To sum up, listwise deletion is not a *bad* method for handling missing data. Although it does not use all of the available information, at least it gives valid inferences when the data are MCAR. As we will see, that is more than can be said for nearly all the other commonplace methods for handling missing data. The methods of maximum likelihood and multiple imputation, discussed in later chapters, are potentially much better than listwise deletion in many situations, but for regression analysis, listwise deletion is even more robust than these sophisticated methods to violations of the MAR assumption. Specifically, whenever the probability of missing data on a particular independent variable depends on the value of that variable (and not the dependent variable), listwise deletion may do better than maximum likelihood or multiple imputation.

There is one important caveat to these claims about listwise deletion for regression analysis. The regression coefficients are assumed to be the same for all cases in the sample. If the regression coefficients vary across subsets of the population, then any nonrandom restriction of the sample (e.g., through listwise deletion) may weight the regression coefficients toward one subset or another. Of course, if such variation in the regression parameters is suspected, either separate regressions should be done in different subsamples or appropriate interactions should be included in the regression model (Winship & Radbill, 1994).

Pairwise Deletion

Also known as available case analysis, pairwise deletion is a simple alternative that can be used for many linear models, including linear regression, factor analysis, and more complex structural equation models. It is well known, for example, that a linear regression can be estimated using only the sample means and covariance matrix or, equivalently, the means, standard deviations, and correlation matrix. The idea of pairwise deletion is to compute each of these summary statistics using all the cases that are available. For example, to compute the covariance between two variables X and Z, all the cases that have data present for both X and Z are used. Once the summary measures have been computed, they can be used to calculate the parameters of interest, for example, regression coefficients.

There are ambiguities in how to implement this principle. When computing a covariance that requires the mean for each variable, do you compute the means using only cases with data on both variables or do you compute them from all the available cases on each variable? There is no point to dwelling on such questions because all the variations lead to estimators with similar properties. The general conclusion is that if the data are MCAR, pairwise deletion produces parameter estimates that are consistent (and, therefore, approximately unbiased in large samples). On the other hand, if the data are only MAR, but not observed at random, the estimates may be seriously biased.

If the data are indeed MCAR, pairwise deletion might be expected to be more efficient than listwise deletion because more information is utilized. By more efficient, I mean that the pairwise estimates would have less sampling variability (smaller true standard errors) than the listwise estimates. This is not always true, however. Both analytical and simulation studies of linear regression models indicate that pairwise deletion produces more efficient estimates when the correlations among the variables are generally low, whereas listwise deletion does better when the correlations are high (Glasser, 1964; Haitovsky, 1968; Kim & Curry, 1977).

The big problem with pairwise deletion is that the estimated standard errors and test statistics produced by conventional software are biased. Symptomatic of that problem is that when you input a covariance matrix to a regression program, you must also specify the sample size to calculate standard errors. Some programs for pairwise deletion use the number of cases on the variable with the most missing data, whereas others use the minimum of the number of cases used to compute each covariance. No single number is satisfactory, however. In principle, it is possible to get consistent estimates of the standard errors, but the formulas are complex and have not been implemented in any commercial software.[3]

A second problem that occasionally arises with pairwise deletion, especially in small samples, is that the constructed covariance or correlation matrix may not be "positive definite," which implies that the regression computations cannot be carried out at all. Because of these difficulties, as well as its relative sensitivity to departures from MCAR, pairwise deletion cannot be generally recommended as an alternative to listwise deletion.

Dummy Variable Adjustment

There is another method for missing predictors in a regression analysis that is remarkably simple and intuitively appealing (Cohen & Cohen, 1985). Suppose that some data are missing on a variable X, which is one of several independent variables in a regression analysis. We create a dummy variable D that is equal to 1 if data are missing on X and equal to 0 otherwise. We also create a variable X^* such that

$$X^* = \begin{cases} X & \text{when data are not missing,} \\ c & \text{when data are missing,} \end{cases}$$

where c can be any constant. We then regress the dependent variable Y on X^*, D, and any other variables in the intended model. This technique, known as dummy variable adjustment or the missing-indicator method, can be extended easily to the case of more than one independent variable with missing data.

The apparent virtue of the dummy variable adjustment method is that it uses all the information that is available about the missing data. Substitution of the value c for the missing data is not properly regarded as imputation because the coefficient of X^* is invariant to the choice of c. Indeed, the only aspect of the model that depends on the choice of c is the coefficient of D, the missing value indicator. For ease of interpretation, a convenient choice of c is the mean of X for nonmissing cases. Then the coefficient of D can be interpreted as the predicted value of Y for individuals with missing data on X minus the predicted value of Y for individuals at the mean of X, controlling for other variables in the model. The coefficient for X^* can be regarded as an estimate of the effect of X among the subgroup of those that have data on X.

Unfortunately, this method generally produces biased estimates of the coefficients, as proven by Jones (1996).[4] A simple simulation illustrates the problem. I generated 10,000 cases on three variables, X, Y, and Z, by sampling from a trivariate normal distribution. For the regression of Y on X and Z, the true coefficients for each variable were 1.0. For the full sample of 10,000, the least-squares regression coefficients, shown in the first column of Table 3.1 are—not surprisingly—quite close to the true values.

I then randomly made some of the Z values missing with a probability of 1/2. Because the probability of missing data is unrelated to any other variable, the data are MCAR. The second column in Table 3.1 shows that listwise deletion yields estimates that are very close to those obtained when no data are missing. On the other hand, the coefficients for the dummy variable adjustment method are

TABLE 3.1
Regression in Simulated Data for Three Methods

Coefficient of	Full Data	Listwise Deletion	Dummy Variable Adjustment
X	0.98	0.96	1.28
Z	1.01	1.03	0.87
D			0.02

clearly biased—too high for the X coefficient and too low for the Z coefficient.

A closely related method has been proposed for categorical independent variables in regression analysis. Such variables are typically handled by creating a set of dummy variables, one variable for each of the categories except for a reference category. The proposal is simply to create an additional category—and an additional dummy variable—for those individuals with missing data on the categorical variables. Again, however, we have an intuitively appealing method that is biased even when the data are MCAR (Jones, 1996; Vach and Blettner, 1991).

Imputation

Many missing data methods fall under the general heading of imputation. The basic idea is to substitute some reasonable guess (imputation) for each missing value and then proceed to do the analysis as if there were no missing data. Of course, there are lots of different ways to impute missing values. Perhaps the simplest is marginal mean imputation: For each missing value on a given variable, substitute the mean for those cases with data present on that variable. This method is well known to produce biased estimates of variances and covariances (Haitovsky, 1968) and generally should be avoided.

A better approach is to use information on other variables by way of multiple regression, a method sometimes known as conditional mean imputation. Suppose we are estimating a multiple regression model with several independent variables. One of those variables, X, has missing data for some of the cases. For those cases with complete data, we regress X on all the other independent variables. Using the estimated equation, we generate predicted values for the cases with missing data on X. These are substituted for the missing data and the analysis proceeds as if there were no missing data.

The method gets more complicated when more than one independent variable has missing data, and there are several variations on the general theme. In general, if imputations are based solely on other independent variables (not the dependent variable) and if the data are MCAR, the least-squares coefficients are consistent, implying that they are approximately unbiased in large samples (Gourieroux & Monfort, 1981). However, they are not fully efficient. Improved estimators can be obtained using weighted least squares (Beale & Little, 1975) or generalized least squares (Gourieroux & Monfort, 1981).

Unfortunately, all of these imputation methods suffer from a fundamental problem: Analyzing imputed data as though it were complete data produces standard errors that are underestimated and test statistics that are overestimated. Conventional analytic methods simply do not adjust for the fact that the imputation process involves uncertainty about the missing values.[5] In later chapters, an approach to imputation that overcomes these difficulties is examined.

Summary

All the common methods for salvaging information from cases with missing data typically make things worse: They introduce substantial bias, make the analysis more sensitive to departures from MCAR, or yield standard error estimates that are incorrect (usually too low). In light of these shortcomings, listwise deletion does not look so bad. However, better methods are available. In the next chapter, maximum likelihood methods that are available for many common modeling objectives are examined. In Chapters 5 and 6, multiple imputation, which can be used in almost any setting, is considered. Both methods have very good properties if the data are MAR. In principle, these methods also can be used for nonignorable missing data, but that requires a correct model of the process by which data are missing— something that usually is difficult to come by.

4. MAXIMUM LIKELIHOOD

Maximum likelihood (ML) is a very general approach to statistical estimation that is widely used to handle many otherwise difficult estimation problems. Most readers will be familiar with ML as the preferred method for estimating the logistic regression model. Ordinary least-squares linear regression is also an ML method when the error term is assumed to be normally distributed. It turns out that ML is particularly adept at handling missing data problems. In this chapter, I begin by reviewing some general properties of ML estimates. Then I present the basic principles of ML estimation under the assumption that the missing data mechanism is ignorable. These principles are illustrated with a simple contingency table example. The remainder of the chapter considers more complex examples where the goal is to estimate a linear model, based on the multivariate normal distribution.

Review of Maximum Likelihood

The basic principle of ML estimation is to choose as estimates those values that, if true, would maximize the probability of observing what has, in fact, been observed. To accomplish this, we first need a formula that expresses the probability of the data as a function of both the data and the unknown parameters. When observations are independent (the usual assumption), the overall likelihood (probability) for the sample is just the product of all the likelihoods for the individual observations.

Suppose we are trying to estimate a parameter θ. If $f(y|\theta)$ is the probability (or probability density) of observing a single value of Y given some value of θ, the likelihood for a sample of n observations is

$$L(\theta) = \prod_{i=1}^{n} f(y_i|\theta),$$

where $\prod$ is the symbol for repeated multiplication. Of course, we still need to specify exactly what $f(y|\theta)$ is. For example, suppose Y is a dichotomous variable coded 1 or 0, and θ is the probability that $Y = 1$. Then

$$L(\theta) = \prod_{i=1}^{n} \theta^{y_i}(1 - \theta)^{1-y_i}.$$

Once we have $L(\theta)$—which is called the likelihood function—there are a variety of techniques to find the value of θ that makes the likelihood as large as possible.

ML estimators have a number of desirable properties. Under a fairly wide range of conditions, they are known to be consistent, asymptotically efficient, and asymptotically normal (Agresti & Finlay, 1997). Consistency implies that the estimates are approximately unbiased in large samples. Efficiency implies that the true standard errors are at least as small as the standard errors for any other consistent estimators. The asymptotic part means that this statement is only approximately true, and the approximation gets better as the sample size gets larger. Finally, asymptotic normality means that in repeated sampling, the estimates have an approximately normal distribution (again, the approximation improves with increasing sample size). This justifies the use of a normal table to construct confidence intervals or compute p values.

ML With Missing Data

What happens when data are missing for some of the observations? When the missing data mechanism is ignorable (and hence MAR), we can obtain the likelihood simply by summing the usual likelihood over all possible values of the missing data. Suppose, for example, that we attempt to collect data on two variables, X and Y, for a sample of n independent observations. For the first m observations, we observe both X and Y, but for the remaining $n - m$ observations, we are only able to measure Y. For a single observation with complete data, let us represent the likelihood by $f(x, y|\theta)$, where θ is a set of unknown parameters that govern the distribution of X and Y. Assuming that X is discrete, the likelihood for a case with missing data on X is just the "marginal" distribution of Y:

$$g(y|\theta) = \sum_x f(x, y|\theta).$$

(When X is continuous, the summation is replaced by an integral.) The likelihood for the entire sample is just

$$L(\theta) = \prod_{i=1}^{m} f(x_i, y_i|\theta) \prod_{i=m+1}^{n} g(y_i|\theta).$$

The problem then becomes one of finding values of θ to make this likelihood as large as possible. A variety of methods are available to solve this optimization problem, and a few of them will be considered later.

ML is particularly easy when the pattern of missing data is *monotonic*. In a monotonic pattern, the variables can be arranged in an order such that for any observation in the sample, if data are missing on a particular variable, they also must be missing for all variables that come later in the order. Here is an example with four variables, X_1, X_2, X_3, and X_4. There are no missing data on X_1. Ten percent of the cases are missing on X_2. Those cases that are missing on X_2 also have missing data on X_3 and X_4. An additional 20% of the cases have missing data on both X_3 and X_4, but not on X_2. A monotonic pattern often arises in panel studies, where people drop out at various points in time and never return.

If only one variable has missing data, the pattern is necessarily monotonic. Consider the two-variable case with data missing on X only. The joint distribution $f(x, y)$ can be written as $h(x|y)g(y)$, where $g(y)$ is the marginal distribution of Y (previously defined) and $h(x|y)$ is the conditional distribution of X given Y. This enables us to rewrite the likelihood as

$$L(\lambda, \phi) = \prod_{i=1}^{m} h(x_i|y_i; \lambda) \prod_{i=1}^{n} g(y_i|\phi).$$

This expression differs from the earlier one in two important ways. First, the second product is over *all* the observations, not just those with missing data on X. Second, the parameters have been separated into two parts: λ describes the conditional distribution of X given Y and ϕ describes the marginal distribution of Y. These changes imply that we can maximize the two parts of the likelihood separately, typically using conventional estimation procedures for each part. Thus, if X and Y have a bivariate normal distribution, we can calculate the mean and variance of Y for the entire sample. Then, for those cases with data on X, we can calculate the regression of X on Y. The resulting parameter estimates can be combined to produce ML estimates for any other parameters we might be interested in, for example, the correlation coefficient.

Contingency Table Data

These features of ML estimation can be illustrated very concretely with contingency table data. Suppose for a simple random sample of 200 people, we attempt to measure two dichotomous variables, X and Y, with possible values of 1 and 2. For 150 cases, we observe both X and Y, and obtain the results shown in the following contingency table:

	$Y=1$	$Y=2$
$X=1$	52	21
$X=2$	34	43

For the other 50 cases, X is missing and we observe only Y; specifically, we have 19 cases with $Y = 1$ and 31 cases with $Y = 2$. In the population, the relationship between X and Y is described by

	$Y=1$	$Y=2$
$X=1$	p_{11}	p_{12}
$X=2$	p_{21}	p_{22}

where p_{ij} is the probability that $X = i$ and $Y = j$. If all we had were the 150 observations with complete data, the likelihood would be

$$L = (p_{11})^{52}(p_{12})^{21}(p_{21})^{34}(p_{22})^{43},$$

subject to the constraint that the four probabilities must sum to 1. The ML estimates of the four probabilities would be the simple proportions in each cell, that is,

$$\hat{p}_{ij} = \frac{n_{ij}}{n},$$

where n_{ij} is the number of cases that fall into cell (i, j). So we would get

$$\hat{p}_{11} = .346,$$
$$\hat{p}_{21} = .227,$$
$$\hat{p}_{12} = .140,$$
$$\hat{p}_{22} = .287.$$

However, this will not do because we have additional observations on Y alone that need to be incorporated into the likelihood. Assuming that the missing data mechanism is ignorable, the likelihood for cases with $Y = 1$ is just $p_{11} + p_{21}$, the marginal probability that $Y = 1$. Similarly, for cases with $Y = 2$, the likelihood is $p_{12} + p_{22}$. Thus, our likelihood for the entire sample is

$$L = (p_{11})^{52}(p_{12})^{21}(p_{21})^{34}(p_{22})^{43}(p_{11} + p_{21})^{19}(p_{12} + p_{22})^{31}.$$

How can we find values of p_{ij} that maximize this expression? For most applications of ML to missing data problems, there is no explicit solution for the estimates. Instead, iterative methods are necessary. In this case, however, the pattern is necessarily monotonic (because there is only one variable with missing data), so we can estimate the conditional distribution of X given Y and the marginal distribution of Y separately. Then we combine the results to get the four cell probabilities. For the 2×2 table, the ML estimates have the general form

$$\hat{p}_{ij} = \hat{p}(X = i | Y = j)\hat{p}(Y = j).$$

The conditional probabilities on the right-hand side are estimated using only those cases with complete data. They are obtained in the usual way by dividing the cell frequencies in the 2×2 table by the column totals. The estimates of the marginal probabilities for Y are obtained by adding the column frequencies to the frequencies of Y for the cases with missing data on X and then dividing by the sample size. Thus, we have

$$\hat{p}_{11} = \left(\frac{52}{86}\right)\left(\frac{86+19}{200}\right) = .3174,$$

$$\hat{p}_{21} = \left(\frac{34}{86}\right)\left(\frac{86+19}{200}\right) = .2076,$$

$$\hat{p}_{12} = \left(\frac{21}{64}\right)\left(\frac{64+31}{200}\right) = .1559,$$

$$\hat{p}_{22} = \left(\frac{43}{64}\right)\left(\frac{64+31}{200}\right) = .3191.$$

Of course, these estimates are not the same as if we had used only the cases with complete information. On the other hand, the *cross-product ratio*, a commonly used measure of association for two dichotomous variables, is the same whether it is calculated from the ML estimates or the estimates based on complete cases only. In short, the observations with missing data on X give us no additional information about the cross-product ratio.

This example was included to illustrate some of the general features of ML estimation with missing data. Few readers will want to work through the hand calculations for their particular applications, however. What is needed is general-purpose software that can handle a variety of data types and missing data patterns. Although ML estimation for the analysis of contingency tables is not computationally difficult (Fuchs, 1982; Schafer, 1997), there is virtually no commercial software to handle this case. Freeware is available on the Web, however:

- Jeroen K. Vermunt's ℓ_{EM} program for Windows (http://www.kub.nl/ faculteiten/fsw/organisatie/departementen/mto/software2.html) estimates a wide variety of categorical data models when some data are missing.
- Joseph Schafer's CAT program (http://www.stat.psu.edu/~jls) will estimate hierarchical log-linear models with missing data, but is currently available only as a library for the S-PLUS package.
- David Duffy's LOGLIN program will estimate a variety of log-linear models with missing data (http://www2.qimr.edu.au/davidD).

Linear Models With Normally Distributed Data

ML can be used to estimate a variety of linear models under the assumption that the data come from a multivariate normal distribution. Possible models include ordinary linear regression, factor analysis, simultaneous equations, and structural equations with latent variables. Although the assumption of multivariate normality is a strong one, it is completely innocuous for those variables with no missing data. Furthermore, even when some variables with missing data are known to have distributions that are not normal (e.g., dummy variables), ML estimates under the multivariate normal assumption often have good properties, especially if the data are MCAR.[6]

There are several approaches to ML estimation for multivariate normal data with an ignorable missing data mechanism. When the missing data follow a monotonic pattern, use can be made of the approach described earlier of factoring the likelihood into conditional and marginal distributions that can be estimated by conventional software (Marini, Olsen, & Rubin, 1979). However, this approach is very restricted in terms of potential applications, and it is not easy to get good estimates of standard errors and test statistics.

General missing data patterns can be handled by a method called the expectation–maximization (EM) algorithm (Dempster, Laird, & Rubin, 1977), which can produce ML estimates of the means, standard deviations, and correlations (or, equivalently, the means and the covariance matrix). These summary statistics then can be input to standard linear modeling software to get consistent estimates of the parameters of interest. The virtues of the EM method are (1) it is easy to use and (2) there is a lot of software, both commercial and freeware, that will do it. The two disadvantages are (1) standard errors and test statistics reported by the linear modeling software will not be correct, and (2) the estimates will not be fully efficient for overidentified models (those that imply restrictions on the covariance matrix).

A better approach is direct maximization of the multivariate normal likelihood for the assumed linear model. Direct ML (sometimes called raw maximum likelihood) gives efficient estimates with correct standard errors, but requires specialized software that may have a steep learning curve. In the remainder of this chapter, we'll see how to use both the EM algorithm and direct ML.

The EM Algorithm

The EM algorithm is a very general method for obtaining ML estimates when some of the data are missing (Dempster et al., 1977, McLachlan & Krishnan, 1997). It is called EM because it consists of two steps: an *expectation* step and a *maximization* step. These two steps are repeated multiple times in an iterative process that eventually converges to the ML estimates.

Instead of explaining the two steps of the EM algorithm in general settings, I'm going to focus on its application to the multivariate normal distribution. Here the E step essentially reduces to regression imputation of the missing values. Suppose our data set contains four variables, X_1 through X_4, and there are some missing data on each variable, in no particular pattern. We begin by choosing starting values for the unknown parameters, that is, the means and the covariance matrix. These starting values can be obtained by the standard formulas for sample means and covariances, using either listwise deletion or pairwise deletion. Based on the starting values of the parameters, we can compute coefficients for the regression of any one of the Xs on any subset of the other three. For example, suppose that some of the cases have data present for X_1 and X_2, but not for X_3 and X_4. We use the starting values of the covariance matrix to get the regression of X_3 on X_1 and X_2 and the regression of X_4 on X_1 and X_2. We then use these regression coefficients to generate imputed values for X_3 and X_4 based on observed values of X_1 and X_2. For cases with missing data on only one variable, we use regression imputations based on all three of the other variables.

After all the missing data have been imputed, the M step consists of calculating new values for the means and the covariance matrix, using the imputed data along with the nonmissing data. For means, we just use the usual formula. For variances and covariances, modified formulas must be used for any terms that involve missing data. Specifically, terms must be added that correspond to the residual variances and residual covariances, based on the regression equations used in the imputation process. For example, suppose that for observation i, X_3 was imputed using X_1 and X_2. Then, whenever $(x_{i3})^2$ would have been used in the conventional variance formula, we substitute $(x_{i3})^2 + s_{3\cdot21}^2$, where $s_{3\cdot21}^2$ is the residual variance from regressing X_3 on X_1 and X_2. The addition of the residual terms corrects for the usual underestimation of variances that occurs in more conventional imputation schemes. Suppose X_4 is also missing for observation i. Then, when computing the covariance between X_3 and X_4, wherever $x_{i3}x_{i4}$ would have been used in the conventional covariance formula, we substitute $x_{i3}x_{i4} + s_{34\cdot21}$. The last term is the residual covariance between X_3 and X_4, controlling for X_1 and X_2.

Once we have gotten new estimates for the means and covariance matrix, we start over with the E step. That is, we use the new estimates to produce new regression imputations for the missing values. We keep cycling through the E and M steps until the estimates converge, that is, they hardly change from one iteration to the next.

Note that the EM algorithm avoids one of the difficulties with conventional regression imputation—deciding which variables to use as predictors and coping with the fact that different missing data patterns have different sets of available predictors. Because EM always starts with the full covariance matrix, it is possible to get regression estimates for any set of predictors, no matter how few cases there may be in a particular missing data pattern. Hence, EM always uses all the available variables as predictors for imputing the missing data.

21

EM Example

Data on 1,302 American colleges and universities were reported in the *U.S. News and World Report Guide to America's Best Colleges 1994*. These data can be found on the Web at http://lib.stat.cmu.edu/datasets/colleges. We consider the following variables:

GRADRAT Ratio of graduating seniors to number that enrolled four years earlier ($\times 100$).

CSAT Combined average scores on verbal and math sections of the SAT.

LENROLL Natural logarithm of the number of enrolling freshmen.

PRIVATE 1=private; 0=public.

STUFAC Ratio of students to faculty ($\times 100$).

RMBRD Total annual costs for room and board (thousands of dollars).[7]

ACT Mean ACT scores.

Our goal is to estimate a linear regression of GRADRAT on the next five variables. Although ACT will not be in the regression model, it is included in the EM estimation because of its high correlation with CSAT, a variable that has substantial missing data, which allows us to get better imputations for the missing values.

Table 4.1 gives the number of nonmissing cases for each variable, and the means and standard deviations for those cases with data present. Only one variable, PRIVATE, has complete data. The

TABLE 4.1
Descriptive Statistics for College Data Based on Available Cases

Variable	Nonmissing Cases	Mean	Standard Deviation
GRADRAT	1,204	60.41	18.89
CSAT	779	967.98	123.58
LENROLL	1,297	6.17	1.00
PRIVATE	1,302	0.64	0.48
STUFAC	1,300	14.89	5.19
RMBRD	783	4.15	1.17
ACT	714	22.12	2.58

TABLE 4.2
Regression That Predicts GRADRAT Using Listwise Deletion

Variable	Coefficient	Standard Error	t Statistic	p Value
INTERCEP	−35.028	7.685	−4.56	0.0001
CSAT	0.067	0.006	10.47	0.0001
LENROLL	2.417	0.959	2.52	0.0121
PRIVATE	13.588	1.946	6.98	0.0001
STUFAC	−0.123	0.132	−0.93	0.3513
RMBRD	2.162	0.714	3.03	0.0026

dependent variable GRADRAT has missing data on 8% of the colleges. CSAT and RMBRD are each missing 40% and ACT is missing 45% of the cases. Using listwise deletion on all variables except ACT yields a sample of only 455 cases, a clearly unacceptable reduction. Nevertheless, for the purposes of comparison, listwise deletion regression estimates are presented in Table 4.2.

Next we use the EM algorithm to get estimates of the means, standard deviations, and correlations. Among major commercial packages, the EM algorithm is available in BMDP, SPSS, SYSTAT, and SAS. However, with SPSS and SYSTAT, it is cumbersome to save the results for input to other linear modeling routines. For the college data, I used the SAS procedure MI to obtain the results shown in Tables 4.3 and 4.4. Like other EM software, this procedure automates all the steps described in the previous section.

Comparison of the means in Table 4.3 with those in Table 4.1 indicates that the biggest differences are found—not surprisingly—

TABLE 4.3
Means and Standard Deviations
From the EM Algorithm

Variable	Mean	Standard Deviation
GRADRAT	59.86	18.86
CSAT	957.88	121.43
LENROLL	6.17	0.997
PRIVATE	0.64	0.48
STUFAC	14.86	5.18
RMBRD	4.07	1.15
ACT	22.22	2.71

TABLE 4.4
Correlations From the EM Algorithm

	GRADRAT	CSAT	LENROLL	PRIVATE	STUFAC	RMBRD	ACT
GRADRAT	1.000						
CSAT	0.591	1.000					
LENROLL	−0.027	0.192	1.000				
PRIVATE	0.398	0.161	−0.619	1.000			
STUFAC	−0.318	−0.315	0.267	−0.368	1.000		
RMBRD	0.478	0.479	−0.016	0.340	−0.282	1.000	
ACT	0.598	0.908	0.174	0.224	−0.293	0.484	1.000

among the variables with the most missing data: GRADRAT, CSAT, RMBRD, and ACT. However, even for these variables, none of the differences between listwise deletion and EM exceeds 2%.

Table 4.5 shows regression estimates that use the EM statistics as input. Although the coefficients are not markedly different from those in Table 4.2, which used listwise deletion, the reported standard errors are much lower, leading to higher t statistics and lower p values. Unfortunately, although the coefficients are true ML estimates in this case, the standard error estimates are undoubtedly too low because they assume that there are complete data for all the cases. To get correct standard error estimates, we will use the direct ML method, which is described next.[8]

Direct ML

As we have just seen, most software for the EM algorithm produces estimates of the means and an unrestricted correlation (or covariance)

TABLE 4.5
Regression That Predicts GRADRAT Based on the EM Algorithm

Variable	Coefficient	Standard Error	t Statistic	p Value
INTERCEP	−32.395	4.355	−7.44	0.0001
CSAT	0.067	0.004	17.15	0.0001
LENROLL	2.083	0.539	3.86	0.0001
PRIVATE	12.914	1.147	11.26	0.0001
STUFAC	−0.181	0.084	−2.16	0.0312
RMBRD	2.404	0.400	6.01	0.0001

matrix. When these summary statistics are input to other linear models programs, the resulting standard error estimates will be biased, usually downward. To do better, we need to maximize the likelihood function for the model of interest directly. This can be accomplished with any one of several software packages for estimating structural equation models (SEMs) with latent variables.

When there are only a small number of missing data patterns, linear models can be estimated with any SEM program that will handle multiple groups (Allison, 1987; Muthén, Kaplan, & Hollis, 1987), including LISREL and EQS. For more general patterns of missing data, there are currently four programs that perform direct ML estimation of linear models:

Amos   A commercial program for SEM modeling that is available as a stand-alone package or as a module for SPSS. Information is available at http://www.smallwaters.com.

Mplus   A stand-alone commercial program. Information is available at http://www.statmodel.com.

LINCS   A commercial module for Gauss. Information is available at http://www.aptech.com≠3party.html.

Mx   A freeware program available for download at http://views.vcu.edu/mx.

Before proceeding to an example, let us consider a bit of the underlying theory. Let $f(\mathbf{x}|\boldsymbol{\mu}, \boldsymbol{\Sigma})$ be the multivariate normal density for an observed vector $\mathbf{x}$, mean vector $\boldsymbol{\mu}$, and covariance matrix $\boldsymbol{\Sigma}$. If we had complete data for a sample of $i = 1, \ldots, n$ observations from this multivariate normal population, the likelihood function would be

$$L(\boldsymbol{\mu}, \boldsymbol{\Sigma}) = \prod_i f(\mathbf{x}_i|\boldsymbol{\mu}, \boldsymbol{\Sigma}).$$

Suppose we do not have complete data. If data are missing on some variables for case i, we now let $\mathbf{x}_i$ be a smaller vector that simply deletes the missing elements from $\mathbf{x}$. Let $\boldsymbol{\mu}_i$ be the subvector of $\boldsymbol{\mu}$ that deletes the corresponding elements that are missing from $\mathbf{x}_i$ and let $\boldsymbol{\Sigma}_i$ be a submatrix of $\boldsymbol{\Sigma}$ formed by deleting the rows and column that correspond to missing values of $\mathbf{x}$. Our likelihood function then becomes

$$L(\boldsymbol{\mu}, \boldsymbol{\Sigma}) = \prod_i f(\mathbf{x}_i|\boldsymbol{\mu}_i, \boldsymbol{\Sigma}_i).$$

Although this function looks simple enough, it is considerably more difficult to work with than the likelihood function for complete data. Nevertheless, this likelihood function can be maximized using conventional approaches to ML estimation. In particular, we can take the logarithm of the likelihood function, differentiate it with respect to the unknown parameters, and set the result equal to 0. The resulting equations can be solved by numerical algorithms like the Newton–Raphson method, which produces standard errors as a by-product. It is also possible to impose a structure on μ and Σ by letting them be functions of a smaller set of parameters that correspond to some assumed linear model, for example, the factor model sets

$$\Sigma = \Lambda \Phi \Lambda' + \Psi,$$

where Λ is a matrix of factor loadings, Φ is the covariance matrix of the latent factors, and Ψ is the covariance matrix of the error components. The estimation process can produce ML estimates of these parameters along with standard error estimates.

Direct ML Example

I estimated the college regression model using Amos 3.6, which has both a graphical user interface and a text interface. The graphical interface allows the user to specify equations by drawing arrows among the variables. Because I can not show you a real-time demonstration, the equivalent text commands are shown in Figure 4.1. The data were in a free-format text file called COLLEGE.DAT, with missing values denoted by −9. The $mstructure command tells Amos to estimate means for the specified variables, an essential part of estimating models with missing data. The $structure command specifies the equation to be estimated. The parentheses immediately after the equals sign indicate that an intercept is to be estimated. The (1) error at the end of the line tells Amos to include an error term with a coefficient of 1.0. The last line, act < > error, allows for a correlation between ACT and the error term, which is possible because ACT has no direct effect on GRADRAT. Amos automatically allows for correlations between ACT and the other independent variables in the regression equation.

Results are shown in Table 4.6. A comparison of these results with the two-step EM estimates in Table 4.5 shows that the coefficient

```
$Sample size = 1302
$missing = -9
$input variables
  gradrat
  csat
  lenroll
  private
  stufac
  rmbrd
  act
$rawdata
$include=c:\college.dat
$mstructure
  csat
  lenroll
  private
  stufac
  rmbrd
  act
$structure
  gradrat = () + csat + lenroll + private + stufac
             + rmbrd + (1) error
  act<>error
```

Figure 4.1. Amos Commands for the Regression Model That Predicts GRADRAT

estimates are identical, but the Amos standard errors are noticeably larger—which is just what we would expect. They are still quite a bit smaller than those in Table 4.2 that were obtained with listwise deletion.

Conclusion

Maximum likelihood can be an effective and practical method for handling data that are missing at random. In this situation, ML estimates are known to be optimal in large samples. For linear models that fall within the general class of structural equation models estimated by programs like LISREL, ML estimates are easily obtained

TABLE 4.6
Regressions That Predict GRADRAT Using Direct ML With Amos

Variable	Coefficient	Standard Error	t Statistic	p Value
INTERCEPT	−32.395	4.863	−6.661	0.000000
CSAT	0.067	0.005	13.949	0.000000
LENROLL	2.083	0.595	3.499	0.000467
PRIVATE	12.914	1.277	10.114	0.000000
STUFAC	−0.181	0.092	−1.968	0.049068
RMBRD	2.404	0.548	4.386	0.000012

by several widely available software packages. Software is also available for ML estimation of log-linear models for categorical data, but the implementation in this setting is somewhat less straightforward. One limitation of the ML approach is that it requires a model for the joint distribution of all variables with missing data. The multivariate normal model is often convenient for this purpose, but may be unrealistic for many applications.

5. MULTIPLE IMPUTATION: BASICS

Although ML represents a major advance over conventional approaches to missing data, it has its limitations. As we have seen, ML theory and software are readily available for linear models and log-linear models, but beyond that, either theory or software is generally lacking. For example, if you want to estimate a Cox proportional hazards model or an ordered logistic regression model, you will have a tough time implementing ML methods for missing data. Even if your model *can* be estimated with ML, you will need to use specialized software that may lack diagnostics or graphical output that you particularly want.

Fortunately, there is an alternative approach—multiple imputation—that has the same optimal properties as ML, but removes some of these limitations. More specifically, multiple imputation (MI), when used correctly, produces estimates that are consistent, asymptotically efficient, and asymptotically normal when the data are MAR. Unlike ML, multiple imputation can be used with virtually any kind of data and any kind of model, and the analysis can be done with unmodified, conventional software. Of course MI has its own drawbacks. It can be cumbersome to implement and it is easy to do it the wrong way. Both of these problems can be substantially alleviated by using good software to do the imputations. A more fundamental drawback is that MI produces different estimates (hopefully, only slightly different) every time you use it. That can lead to awkward situations in which different researchers get different numbers from the same data using the same methods.

Single Random Imputation

The reason that MI does not produce a unique set of numbers is that random variation is deliberately introduced in the imputation process. Without a random component, deterministic imputation methods generally produce underestimates of variances for variables with missing data and, sometimes, covariances as well. As we saw in the previous chapter, the EM algorithm for the multivariate normal model solves that problem by using residual variance and covariance estimates to correct the conventional formulas. However, a good alternative is to make random draws from the residual distribution of each imputed variable and add those random numbers to the imputed values. Then, conventional formulas can be used to calculate variances and covariances.

Here is a simple example. Suppose we want to estimate the correlation between X and Y, but data are missing on X for, say, 50% of the cases. We can impute values for the missing Xs by regressing X on Y for the cases with complete data and then using the resulting regression equation to generate predicted values for the cases that are missing on X. I did this for a simulated sample of 10,000 cases, where X and Y were drawn from a standard, bivariate normal distribution with a correlation of 0.30. Half of the X values were assigned to be missing (completely at random). Using the predicted values from the regression of X on Y to substitute for the missing values, the correlation between X and Y was estimated to be 0.42.

Why the overestimate? The sample correlation is just the sample covariance of X and Y divided by the product of their sample standard deviations. The regression imputation method yields unbiased estimates of the covariance. Moreover, the standard deviation of Y(with no missing data) was correctly estimated at about 1.0. However, the standard deviation of X (including the imputed values) was only 0.74, whereas the true standard deviation was 1.0, resulting in an overestimate of the correlation. An alternative way to think about the problem is that the imputed value of X for the 5,000 cases with missing data is a perfect linear function of Y, thereby inflating the correlation between the two variables.

We can correct this bias by taking random draws from the residual distribution of X and then adding these random numbers to the predicted values of X. In this example, the residual distribution of X (regressed on Y) is normal with a mean of 0 and a standard deviation (estimated from the listwise deleted least-squares regression) of 0.9525. For case i, let u_i be a random draw from a standard normal distribution and let $\hat{x}_i$ be the predicted value from the regression of X on Y. Our modified imputed value is then $\tilde{x}_i = \hat{x}_i + 0.9525u_i$. For all observations in which X is missing, we substitute $\tilde{x}_i$ and then compute the correlation. When I did this for the simulated sample of 10,000 cases, the correlation between X (with modified imputed values) and Y was 0.316, only a little higher than the true value of 0.300.

Multiple Random Imputation

Random imputation can eliminate the biases that are endemic to deterministic imputation, but a serious problem remains. If we use imputed data (either random or deterministic) as if it were real data, the resulting standard error estimates generally will be too low and test statistics will be too high. Conventional methods for standard error estimation cannot account adequately for the fact that the data are imputed.

The solution, at least with random imputation, is to repeat the imputation process more than once, producing multiple "completed" data sets. Because of the random component, the estimates of the parameters of interest will be slightly different for each imputed data set. This variability across imputations can be used to adjust the standard errors upward.

For the simulated sample of 10,000 cases, I repeated the random imputation process eight times, yielding the estimates in Table 5.1. Although these estimates are approximately unbiased, the standard errors are downwardly biased because they do not take the imputation[9] into account. We can combine the eight correlation estimates into a single estimate simply by taking their mean, which is 0.3125. An improved estimate of the standard error takes three steps.

TABLE 5.1
Correlations and Standard Errors
for Randomly Imputed Data

Correlation	S.E.
0.3159	0.00900
0.3108	0.00903
0.3135	0.00902
0.3210	0.00897
0.3118	0.00903
0.3022	0.00909
0.3189	0.00898
0.3059	0.00906

1. Square the estimated standard errors (to get variances) and average the results across the eight replications.
2. Calculate the variance of the correlation estimates across the eight replications.
3. Add the results of steps 1 and 2 together (applying a small correction factor to the variance in step 2) and take the square root.

To put this into one formula, let M be the number of replications, let r_k be the correlation in replication k, and let s_k be the estimated standard error in replication k. Then the estimate of the standard error of $\bar{r}$ (the mean of the correlation estimates) is

$$\text{S.E.} (\bar{r}) = \sqrt{\frac{1}{M} \sum_k s_k^2 + \left(1 + \frac{1}{M}\right)\left(\frac{1}{M-1}\right) \sum_k (r_k - \bar{r})^2}. \quad [5.1]$$

This formula can be used for any parameter estimated by multiple imputation, with r_k denoting the kth estimate of the parameter of interest (Rubin, 1987). Applying this formula to the correlation example, we get a standard error of 0.01123, which is about 24% higher than the mean of the standard errors in the eight samples.

Allowing for Random Variation in the Parameter Estimates

Although the method I just described for imputing missing values is pretty good, it is not ideal. To generate the imputations for X, I regressed X on Y for the cases with complete data to produce the regression equation

$$\hat{x}_i = a + by_i.$$

For cases with missing data on X, the imputed values were calculated as

$$\tilde{x}_i = a + by_i + s_{x \cdot y} u_i,$$

where u_i is a random draw from a standard normal distribution and $s_{x \cdot y}$ is the estimated standard deviation of the error term (the root mean squared error). For the simulated data set, we had $a = -0.0015$, $b = 0.3101$, and $s_{x \cdot y} = 0.9525$. These values were used to produce imputations for each of the eight completed data sets.

The problem with this approach is that it treats a, b, and $s_{x \cdot y}$ as though they were the true parameters, not sample estimates. Obviously, we cannot know what the true values are, but for "proper" multiple imputations (Rubin, 1987), each imputed data set should be based on a different set of values of a, b, and $s_{x \cdot y}$. These values should be random draws from the Bayesian posterior distribution of the parameters. Only in this way can multiple imputation completely embody our uncertainty with regard to the unknown parameters.

This claim naturally raises several questions. What is the Bayesian posterior distribution of the parameters? How do we get random draws from the posterior distribution? Do we really need this additional complication? The first question really requires another book and, fortunately, there is a good one in the *Quantitative Applications in the Social Sciences* series (Iversen, 1985). As for the second question, there are several different approaches to getting random draws from the posterior distribution, some of them embodied in easy-to-use software. Later in this chapter, when we consider MI under the multivariate normal model, I will explain one method called data augmentation (Schafer, 1997).

Can you get by without making random draws from the posterior distribution of the parameters? It is important to answer to this question, because some random imputation software—like the missing data module in SPSS—does not randomly draw the parameter values. In many cases, I think the answer is yes. If the sample is large and the proportion of cases with missing data is small, MI without

TABLE 5.2
Correlations and Standard
Errors for Randomly Imputed
Data Using the Data
Augmentation Method

Correlation	S.E.
0.30636	0.0090614
0.31316	0.0090193
0.31837	0.0089864
0.31142	0.0090302
0.32086	0.0089705
0.29760	0.0091143
0.32701	0.0089306
0.30826	0.0090498

this extra step typically will yield results that are very close to those obtained with it. On the other hand, if the sample is small or if the proportion of cases with missing data is large, the additional variation can make a noticeable difference.

Continuing our correlation example, I imputed eight new data sets using the data augmentation method to generate random draws from the posterior distribution of the parameters. Table 5.2 gives the correlation between X and Y, and its standard error for each data set. The mean of the correlation estimates is 0.31288. Using formula 5.1, the estimated standard error is 0.01329, slightly larger than the 0.01123 obtained with the cruder imputation method. In general, the standard errors will be somewhat larger when the parameters used in the imputation are drawn randomly.

Multiple Imputation Under the Multivariate Normal Model

To do multiple imputation, you need a model to generate the imputations. For the two-variable example just considered, I employed a simple regression model with normally distributed errors. Obviously, more complicated situations require more complicated models. As we saw in Chapter 4, maximum likelihood also requires a model. However, MI is probably less sensitive than ML to the choice of model because the model is used only to impute the missing data, not to estimate other parameters.

Ideally, the imputation model would be specially constructed to represent the particular features of each data set. In practice, it is more convenient to work with "off-the-shelf" models that are easy to use and provide reasonably good approximations for a wide range of data sets.

The most popular model for MI is the multivariate normal model, which previously was used in Chapter 4 as the basis for ML estimation of linear models with missing data. The multivariate normal model implies that

- All variables have normal distributions
- Each variable can be represented as a linear function of all the other variables, together with a normal, homoscedastic error term

Although these are strong conditions, in practice the multivariate normal model seems to do a good job of imputation even when some of the variables have distributions that are manifestly not normal (Schafer, 1997). It is a completely innocuous assumption for those variables that have no missing data. For those variables that do have missing data, normalizing transformations can greatly improve the quality of the imputations.

In essence, MI under the multivariate normal model is a generalization of the method used in the two-variable example of the previous section. For each variable with missing data, we estimate the linear regression of that variable on all other variables of interest. Ideally, the regression parameters are random draws from the Bayesian posterior distribution. The estimated regression equations are then used to generate predicted values for the cases with missing data. Finally, to each predicted value, we add a random draw from the residual normal distribution for that variable.

The most complicated part of the imputation process is getting random draws from the posterior distribution of the regression parameters. As of this writing, two algorithms that accomplish this have been implemented in readily available software: data augmentation (Schafer, 1997) and sampling importance/resampling (SIR; Rubin, 1987). Here are some computer programs that implement these methods:

Data Augmentation

> NORM   A freeware package developed by Schafer and described in his 1997 book. Available in either a stand-alone Windows version or as an S-PLUS library (http://www.stat.psu.edu/~jls/).

> SOLAS   A stand-alone commercial package that includes both data augmentation (version 2 and later) and a propensity score method. The latter method is invalid for many applications (Allison, 2000) (http://www.statsolusa.com)

> PROC MI   A SAS procedure available in release 8.1 and later (http://www.sas.com).

Sampling Importance/Resampling

> AMELIA   A freeware package developed by King, Honaker, Joseph, Scheve, and Singh (1999). Available either as a stand-alone Windows program or as a module for Gauss (http://gking.harvard.edu/stats.shtml).

> SIRNORM   A SAS macro written by C. H. Brown and X. Ling (http://yates.coph.usf.edu/research/psmg/web.html).

Both algorithms have some theoretical justification. Proponents of SIR (King, Honaker, Joseph, & Scheve, 2001) claim that it requires far less computer time. However, the relative superiority of these two methods is far from settled. Because I have much more experience with data augmentation, I will focus on this method in the remainder of this chapter.

Data Augmentation for the Multivariate Normal Model

Data augmentation (DA) is a type of Markov chain Monte Carlo (MCMC) algorithm, a general method for finding posterior distributions that has become increasingly popular in Bayesian statistics. In this section, I will describe how it works for the multivariate normal model. Although the available software performs most of the operations automatically, it is helpful to have a general idea of what is going on, especially when things go wrong.

The general structure of the iterative algorithm is much like the EM algorithm for the multivariate normal model, described in the last chapter, except that random draws are made at two points, described subsequently. Before beginning DA, it is necessary to choose a set of variables for the imputation process. Obviously this should include all variables with missing data, as well as other variables in the model to be estimated. It is also worthwhile to include additional variables (not in the intended model) that are highly correlated with the variables that have missing data or that are associated with the probability that those variables have missing data.

Once the variables are chosen, DA consists of the following steps.

1. Choose starting values for the parameters. For the multivariate normal model, the parameters are the means and the covariance matrix. Starting values can be gotten from standard formulas using listwise deletion or pairwise deletion. Even better are the estimates obtained with the EM algorithm described in the last chapter.

2. Use the current values of the means and covariances to obtain estimates of regression coefficients for equations in which each variable with missing data is regressed on all observed variables. This is done for each pattern of missing data.

3. Use the regression estimates to generate predicted values for all the missing values. To each predicted value, add a random draw from the residual normal distribution for that variable.

4. Using the "completed" data set, with both observed and imputed values, recalculate the means and covariance matrix using standard formulas.

5. Based on the newly calculated means and covariances, make a random draw from the posterior distribution of the means and covariances.

6. Using the randomly drawn means and covariances, go back to step 2 and continue cycling through the subsequent steps until convergence is achieved. The imputations that are produced during the final iteration are used to form a completed data set.

Step 5 needs a little more explanation. To get the posterior distribution of the parameters, we first need a "prior" distribution. Although this can be based on prior beliefs about those parameters, the usual practice is to use a "noninformative" prior, that is, a prior distribution that contains little or no information about the parameters. Here is how it works in a simple situation. Suppose we have a sample of size n with measurements on a single, normally distributed variable Y. The sample mean is $\bar{y}$ and the sample variance is s^2. We want random draws from the posterior distribution of μ and σ^2. With a noninformative prior,[10] we can get $\tilde{\sigma}^2$, a random draw for the variance, by sampling from a chi-square distribution with $n - 1$ degrees of freedom, taking the reciprocal of the drawn value, and multiplying the result by ns^2. We then get a random draw for the mean by sampling from a normal distribution with mean $\bar{y}$ and variance $\tilde{\sigma}^2/n$.

If there were no missing data, these would be random draws from the true posterior distribution of the parameters, but if we have imputed any missing data, what we actually have are random draws from the posterior distribution that would result if the imputed data were the true data. Similarly, when we randomly impute missing data in step 3, what we have are random draws from the posterior distribution of the missing data, given the current parameter values. However, because the current values may not be the true values, the imputed data may not be random draws from the true posterior distribution. That is why the procedure must be iterative. By continually moving back and forth between random draws of parameters (conditional on both observed and imputed data) and random draws of the missing data (conditional on the current parameters), we eventually get random draws from the joint posterior distribution of both data and parameters, conditioning only on the observed data.

Convergence in Data Augmentation

When you do data augmentation, you must specify the number of iterations. However, that raises a tough question: How many iterations are necessary to get convergence to the joint posterior distribution of missing data and parameters? With iterative estimation for maximum likelihood, as in the EM algorithm, the estimates converge to a single set of values. Convergence can then be easily assessed by checking to see how much change there is in the parameter estimates from one iteration to the next. For data augmentation, on the other hand, the algorithm converges to a probability distribution, not a single set of values. That makes it rather difficult to determine whether convergence has, in fact, been achieved. Although some diagnostic statistics are available for assessing convergence (Schafer, 1997), they are far from definitive.

In most applications, the choice of number of iterations will be a stab in the dark. To give you some idea of the range of possibilities, Schafer (1997) used anywhere between 50 and 1,000 iterations for the examples in his book. The more the better, but each iteration can be computationally intensive, especially for large samples with lots of variables. Specifying a large number of iterations can leave you staring at your monitor for painfully long periods of time.

There are a couple of principles to keep in mind. First, the higher is the proportion of missing data (actually, missing *information*, which is not quite the same thing), the more iterations will be needed to reach convergence. If only 5% of the cases have any missing data, you can probably get by with only a small number of iterations. Second, the rate of convergence of the EM algorithm is a useful indication of the rate of convergence for data augmentation. A good rule of thumb is that the number of iterations for DA should be at least as large as the number of iterations required for EM. That is another reason for always running EM before data augmentation. (The first reason is that EM gives good starting values for data augmentation.)

My own feeling about the iteration issue is that it is not all that critical in most applications. Moving from deterministic imputation to randomized imputation is a huge improvement, even if the parameters are not randomly drawn. Moving from randomized imputation without random parameter draws to randomized imputation *with* random parameter draws is another substantial improvement, but not nearly as dramatic. Moving from a few iterations of data augmentation to many iterations improves things still further, but the marginal return is likely to be quite small in most applications.

An additional complication stems from the fact that multiple imputation produces multiple data sets. At least two are required, but the more the better. For a fixed amount of computing time, one can either produce more data sets or more iterations of data augmentation per data set. Unfortunately, data sets with lots of missing information need both more iterations and more data sets. Although little has been written about this issue, I tend to think that more priority should be put on additional data sets.

Sequential Versus Parallel Chains of Data Augmentation

We have just seen how to use data augmentation to produce a single, completed data set. For multiple imputation, we need several data sets. Two methods have been proposed to do this:

1. *Parallel.* Run a separate chain of iterations for each of the desired data sets. These might be from the same set of starting values (say, the EM estimates) or different starting values.

2. *Sequential.* Run one long chain of data augmentation cycles. Take the imputations produced in every kth iteration, where k is chosen to give the desired number of data sets. For example, if we want five data sets, we could first run 500 iterations and then use the imputations produced by every 100th iteration. The larger number of 500 iterations before the first imputation constitute a "burn-in" period that allows the process to converge to the correct distribution.

Both methods are acceptable. An advantage of the sequential approach is that convergence to the true posterior distribution is more likely to be achieved, especially for later data sets in the sequence. However, whenever you take multiple data sets from the same chain of iterations, it is questionable whether those data sets are statistically independent, a requirement for valid inference. The closer together two data sets are in the same chain, the more likely there is to be some dependence. That is why you cannot just run 200 iterations to reach convergence and then use the next five iterations to produce five data sets.

The parallel method avoids the problem of dependence, but makes it more questionable whether convergence has been achieved. Furthermore, both Rubin (1987) and Schafer (1997) suggest that instead of using the same set of starting values for each sequence, the starting values should be drawn from an "overdispersed" prior distribution with the EM estimates at the center of that distribution, something that is not always straightforward to do.[11]

For the vast majority of applications, I do not think it makes a substantial difference whether the sequential or parallel method is chosen. With an equal number of iterations, the two methods should give approximately equivalent results. When using the parallel method, I believe that acceptable results can be obtained, in most cases, by using the EM estimates as starting values for each of the iteration chains.

Using the Normal Model for Nonnormal or Categorical Data

Data sets that can be closely approximated by the multivariate normal distribution are rare indeed. Typically, there will be some variables with highly skewed distributions and other variables that are strictly categorical. In such cases, is there any value to the normal-based methods that we have just been considering? As mentioned earlier, there is no problem whatever for variables that have no missing data because nothing is being imputed for them. For variables with missing data, there is a good deal of evidence that these imputation methods can work quite well, even when the distributions are clearly not normal (Schafer, 1997). Nevertheless, there are a few techniques that can improve the performance of the normal model for imputing nonnormal variables.

For quantitative variables that are highly skewed, it is usually helpful to transform the variables to reduce the skewness before doing the imputation. Any transformation that does the job should be OK. After the data have been imputed, the reverse transformation can be applied to bring the variable back to its original metric. For example, the log transformation greatly reduces the skewness for most income data. After imputing, just take the antilog of income. This is particularly helpful for variables that have a restricted range. If you impute the logarithm of income rather than income itself, it is impossible for the imputed values to yield incomes that are less than zero. Similarly, if the variable to be imputed is a proportion, the logit transformation can prevent the imputation of values greater than 1 or less than 0.

Some software can handle the restricted range problem in another way. If you specify a maximum or a minimum value for a particular variable, it will reject all random draws outside that range and simply take additional draws until it gets one within the specified range. Although this is a very useful option, it is still desirable to use transformations that reduce skewness in the variables.

For quantitative variables that are discrete, it is often desirable to round the imputed values to the discrete scale. Suppose, for example, that adults are asked to report how many children they have. This typically will be skewed, so one might begin by applying a logarithmic or square root transformation. After imputation, back transformation will yield numbers with noninteger values. These can be rounded to conform to the original scale. Some software can perform such rounding automatically.

What about variables that are strictly categorical? Although there are methods and computer programs designed strictly for data sets with only categorical variables, as well as for data sets with mixtures of categorical and normally distributed variables, these methods are typically much more difficult to use and often break down completely. Many users will do just as well by applying the normal methods with some minor alterations. Dichotomous variables, such as sex, are usually represented by dummy (indicator) variables with values of 0 or 1. Any transformation of a dichotomy will still yield a dichotomy, so there is no value in trying to reduce skewness. Instead, we can simply impute the 0–1 variable just like any other variable. Then round the imputed values to 0 or 1, according to whether the imputed value is above or below .5. While most imputations will be in the (0, 1) interval, they will sometimes be outside that range. This presents no problem in this case because we simply assign a value of 0 or 1, depending on which is closer to the imputed value.

Variables with more than two categories are usually represented with sets of dummy variables. There is no need to do anything special at the data augmentation stage, but care must be taken when assigning the final values. The problem is that we need to assign individuals to one and only one category, with appropriate coding for the dummy variables. Suppose the variable to be imputed is marital status, which has three categories: never married, currently married, and formerly married. Let N be a dummy variable for never married and let M be a dummy variable for currently married. The imputation is done with these two variables and the imputed values are used to produce final codings. Here are some possible imputations and resulting codings:

Imputed Values			Final Values	
N	M	$1 - N - M$	N	M
.7	.2	.1	1	0
.3	.5	.2	0	1
.2	.2	.6	0	0
.6	.8	−.4	0	1
−.2	.2	1	0	0

The essential rule is this. In addition to the two imputed values, also calculate 1 minus the sum of the two imputed values, which can be regarded as the imputed value for the reference category. Then determine which category has the highest imputed value. If that value corresponds to a category with an explicit dummy variable, assign a value of 1 to that variable. If the highest value corresponds to the reference category, assign a 0 to both dummy variables. Again, although negative values may appear awkward in this context, the rule still can be applied. The extension to four or more categories should be straightforward.

Exploratory Analysis

Typically, much of data analysis consists of exploratory work in which the analyst experiments with different methods and models. For anyone who has done this kind of work, the process of multiple imputation may seem highly problematic. Doing exploratory analysis on several data sets simultaneously would surely be a very cumbersome process. Furthermore, analysis on each data set could suggest a slightly different model, but multiple imputation requires an identical model for all data sets.

The solution is simple, but ad hoc. When generating the multiple data sets, just produce one more data set than you need to do the multiple imputation analysis. Thus, if you want to do multiple imputation on three data sets, then generate four data sets. Use the extra data set to do exploratory analysis. Once you have settled on a single model or a small set of models, reestimate the models on the remaining data sets and apply the methods we have discussed for combining the results. Keep in mind that although the parameter estimates obtained from the exploratory data set will be approximately unbiased, all the standard errors will be biased downward and the test statistics will be biased upward. Consequently, it may be desirable to use somewhat more conservative criteria than usual (with complete data) to judge the adequacy of a given model.

MI Example 1

We now have enough background to consider a realistic example of multiple imputation. Let us revisit the example used in Chapter 4, where the data set consisted of 1,302 American colleges with measurements on seven variables, all but one of which have some missing data. As before, our goal is to estimate a linear regression model that predicts GRADRAT, the ratio of the number of graduating seniors to the number who enrolled as freshman four years earlier. Independent variables include all the others except ACT, the mean of ACT scores. This variable is included in the imputation process to get better predictions of CSAT, the mean of the combined SAT scores. The latter variable has missing data for 40% of the cases, but is highly correlated with ACT for the 488 cases with data present on both variables $(r = .91)$.

The first step was to examine the distributions of the variables to check for normality. Histograms and normal probability plots suggested that all the variables except one had distributions that were reasonably close to a normal distribution. The exception was enrollment, which was highly skewed to the right. As in the ML example, I worked with the natural logarithm of enrollment, which had a distribution with very little skewness.

To do the data augmentation, I used PROC MI in SAS. The first step was to estimate the means, standard deviations, and correlations using the EM algorithm, which were already displayed in Table 4.4. The EM algorithm took 32 iterations to converge. This is a moderately large number, which probably reflects the large percentage of missing data for some of the variables. However, it is not so large as to suggest serious problems in applying either the EM algorithm or data augmentation.

Here is a minimal set of SAS statements to produce the multiple imputations:

```
proc mi data=college out=collimp;
    var gradrat csat lenroll private stufac rmbrd act;
run;
```

college is the name of the input data set (which had periods for missing values) and collimp is the name of the output data set (which contains observed and imputed values). The var statement gives names of variables to be used in the imputation process. The default in PROC MI is to produce five completed data sets based on a sequential chain of iterations. With EM estimates used as starting values, there are 200 "burn-in" iterations before the first imputation. This is followed by 100 iterations between successive imputations. The five data sets are written into one large SAS data set (collimp) to facilitate later analysis. The output data set contains a new variable _imputation_ with values of 1 through 5 to indicate the different data sets. Thus, with 1,302 observations in the original data set, the new data set has 6,510 observations.

Rather than relying on the defaults, I actually used a somewhat more complicated program:

```
proc mi data = my.college out = collimp seed = 1401
   minimum = 0 600 . . 0 1260 11
   maximum = 100 1410 . . 100 8700 31
   round = 1111. 111;
   var gradrat csat lenroll private stufac rmbrd act;
   MCMC nbiter = 500 niter = 200;
run;
```

seed = 1401 sets a "seed" value for the random number generator so that the results can be exactly reproduced in a later run. The maximum and minimum options set maximum and minimum values for each variable. If a randomly imputed value happens to be outside these bounds, the value is rejected and a new value is drawn. For gradrat and stufac, the maximum and minimum were the theoretical bounds of 0 and 100. For lenroll and private, no bounds were specified. For csat, rmbrd, and act, I used the observed maximum and minimum for each variable. The round option rounds the imputed values of all variables to integers, except for the STUTAC, which is rounded to one decimal place.

The MCMC statement permits more control over the data augmentation process. Here I have specified 500 burn-in iterations before the first imputation, followed by 200 iterations between successive imputations.

Were these enough iterations to achieve convergence? It is hard to say for sure, but we can try out some of the convergence diagnostics suggested by Schafer (1997). One simple approach is to examine some of the parameter values produced at each iteration and see if there is any trend across the iterations. For the multivariate normal model with 7 variables, the parameters are the 7 means, the 7 variances, and the 21 covariances. Rather than examine all the parameters, it is useful to focus on those that involve variables with the most missing data because these are the most likely to be problematic. For these data, the variable CSAT has about 40% missing data. Because the ultimate goal is to estimate the regression that predicts GRADRAT, let us look at the bivariate regression slope for CSAT, which is the covariance of CSAT and GRADRAT divided by the variance of CSAT. Figure 5.1 graphs the values of the regression slope for the first 100 iterations of data augmentation. After the first iteration, there seems

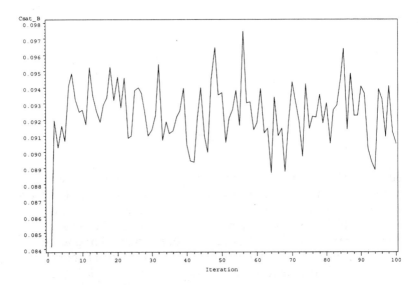

Figure 5.1. Estimates of Regression Slope of GRADRAT on CSAT for the First 100 Iterations of Data Augmentation

to be no particular trend in the estimates of the slope coefficient, which is reassuring.

Another recommended diagnostic is the set of autocorrelations for the parameter of interest at various lags in the sequence of iterations. The objective is to have enough iterations between imputations so that the autocorrelation goes to 0. Using the entire series of 1,300 iterations, Figure 5.2 graphs the autocorrelation between values of the bivariate regression slope for different lags. Thus, the leftmost value of 0.34 represents the correlation between parameter values that are one iteration apart. The second value, 0.13, is the correlation between values that are separated by two iterations. Although these two initial values are high, the autocorrelations quickly settle down to relatively low values (within 0.10 of 0) that have an apparently random pattern. Together these two diagnostics suggest that we could have managed with far fewer than 200 iterations separating the imputations. Nevertheless, it does not hurt to do more, and the diagnostics used here do not guarantee that convergence has been attained.

After producing the completed data sets, I could have transformed the logged enrollment variable back to its original form, but because I

TABLE 5.3
Regression Coefficients (and Standard Errors) for Five Completed Data Sets

Intercept	−33.219	(4.272)	−33.230	(4.250)	−31.256	(4.306)	−34.727	(4.869)	−29.117	(4.924)
CSAT	0.069	(0.004)	0.067	(0.004)	0.071	(0.004)	0.069	(0.004)	0.065	(0.004)
LENROLL	1.550	(0.534)	2.023	(0.526)	1.852	(0.546)	2.187	(0.532)	1.971	(0.538)
PRIVATE	11.632	(1.124)	12.840	(1.126)	12.274	(1.157)	13.468	(1.121)	12.191	(1.141)
STUFAC	−0.145	(0.083)	−0.116	(0.082)	−0.213	(0.084)	−0.142	(0.083)	−0.231	(0.084)
RMBRD	2.951	(0.390)	2.417	(0.392)	1.657	(0.408)	2.103	(0.391)	2.612	(0.393)

45

46

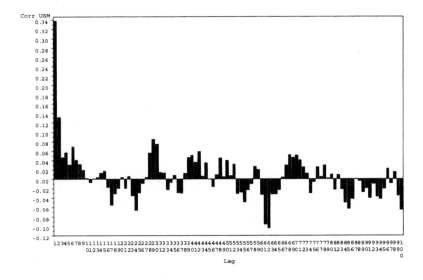

Figure 5.2. Autocorrelations for Regression Slope of GRADRAT on CSAT for Lags Varying Between 1 and 100

expected diminishing returns in the effect of enrollment on graduation rates, I decided to leave the variable in logarithmic form, just as I did for the regression models estimated by ML in Chapter 4. So the next step was simply to estimate the regression model for each of the five completed data sets. This is facilitated in SAS by the use of a BY statement, which avoids the necessity to specify five different regression models:

```
proc reg data = collimp outest = estimate covout;
  model gradrat = csat lenroll private stufac rmbrd;
  by _imputation_;
run;
```

This set of statements tells SAS to estimate a separate regression model for each subgroup defined by the five values of the _imputation_ variable. outest=estimate requests that the regression estimates be written into a new data set called estimate, and covout requests that the covariance matrix of the regression parameters be included in this data set. This makes it easy to combine the estimates in the next step. Results for the five regressions are shown in Table 5.3. Clearly there is a great deal of stability from one regression to the next, but there is also noticeable variability, which is attributable to the random component of the imputation.

The results from these regressions are integrated into a single set of estimates using another SAS procedure called MIANALYZE. It is invoked with the following statements:

```
proc mianalyze data = estimate;
    var intercept csat lenroll private stufac rmbrd;
run;
```

This procedure operates directly on the data set estimate, which contains the coefficients and associated statistics produced by the regressions runs. Results are shown in Figure 5.3.

The column labeled "Mean" in Figure 5.3 contains the means of the coefficients in Table 5.3. The standard errors, calculated using formula 5.1, are appreciably larger than the standard errors in Table 5.3, because the between-regression variability is added to the within-regression variability. However, there is more between-regression variability for some coefficients than for others. At the low end, the standard error for the lenroll coefficient in Figure 5.3 is only about 10% larger than the mean of the standard errors in Table 5.3. At the high end, the combined standard error for rmbrd is about 70% larger than the mean of the individual standard errors. The greater variability in the rmbrd coefficients is apparent in Table 5.3, where the estimates range from 1.66 to 2.95.

The column labeled "t for H0: Mean=0" in Figure 5.3 is just the ratio of each coefficient to its standard error. The immediately preceding column gives the degrees of freedom used to calculate the p value from a t table. This number has nothing to do with the number of observations or the number of variables. It is simply a way to specify a reference distribution that happens to be a good approximation to the sampling distribution of the t-ratio statistic. Although it is not essential to know how the degrees of freedom is calculated, I think it is worth a short explanation. For a given coefficient, let U be the average of the squared, within-regression standard errors. Let B be the variance of the coefficients between regressions. The *relative increase in variance due to missing data* is defined as

$$r = \frac{(1 + M^{-1})B}{U},$$

Multiple-Imputation Parameter Estimates					
Variable	Mean	Std Error Mean	DF	t for H0: Mean= 0	Pr > |t|	Fraction Missing Information
intercept	-32.309795	5.639411	72	-6.596995	<.0001	0.255724
csat	0.068255	0.004692	39	14.547388	<.0001	0.356451
lenroll	1.916654	0.595229	110	3.220027	0.0017	0.206210
private	12.481050	1.367858	40	9.124524	<.0001	0.344151
stufac	-0.169484	0.099331	42	-1.706258	0.0953	0.329284
rmbrd	2.348136	0.670105	10	3.504132	0.0067	0.708476

Figure 5.3. Selected Output From PROC MIANALYZE

where M is, as before, the number of completed data sets used to produce the estimates. The degrees of freedom is then calculated as

$$\text{df} = (M - 1)\left(1 + r^{-1}\right)^2.$$

Thus, the smaller the between-regression variation is relative to the within-regression variation, the larger is the degrees of freedom. Sometimes the calculated degrees of freedom will be substantially greater than the number of observations. This is nothing to be concerned about, because any number greater than about 150 will yield a t table that is essentially the same as a standard normal distribution. However, some software (including **PROC MIANALYZE**) can produce an adjusted degrees of freedom that cannot be greater than the sample size (Barnard & Rubin, 1999).

The last column, "**Fraction Missing Information**," is an estimate of how much information about each coefficient is lost because of missing data. It ranges from a low of 21% for **lenroll** to a high of 71% for **rmbrd**. It's not surprising that the missing information is high for **rmbrd**, which had 40% missing data, but it is surprisingly high for **private**, which had no missing data, and **stufac**, which had less than 1% missing data. To understand this, it is important to know a couple of things. First, the amount of missing information for a given coefficient depends not only on the missing data for that particular variable, but also on the percentage of missing data for other variables that are correlated with it. Second, the MIANALYZE procedure has no way to know how much missing data there are on each variable. Instead, the missing information estimate is based entirely on the relative variation within and between regressions. If there is a lot of variation between regressions, that is an indication of a lot of missing information. Sometimes denoted as γ, the *fraction of missing information* is calculated from two statistics that we just defined, r and df. Ş ᵒcifically,

$$\hat{\gamma} = \frac{r + 2/(\mathrm{df} + 3)}{r + 1}.$$

Keep in mind that the fraction of missing information reported in the table is only an estimate that may be subject to considerable sampling variability.

As noted earlier, one of the troubling things about multiple imputation is that it does not produce a determinate result. Every time you do it, you get slightly different estimates and associated statistics. To see this, take a look at Figure 5.4, which is based on five data

| Multiple-Imputation Parameter Estimates | | | | | | Fraction |
Variable	Mean	Std Error Mean	DF	t for H0: Mean=0	Pr > |t|	Missing Information
intercept	-32.474158	4.816341	124	-6.742496	<.0001	0.192429
csat	0.066590	0.005187	20	12.838386	<.0001	0.489341
lenroll	2.173214	0.546177	2157	3.978955	<.0001	0.043949
private	13.125024	1.171488	1191	11.203719	<.0001	0.059531
stufac	-0.190031	0.099027	51	-1.918988	0.0607	0.307569
rmbrd	2.357444	0.599341	12	3.933396	0.0020	0.623224

Figure 5.4. Output From MIANALYZE for Replication of Multiple Imputation

sets produced by an entirely new run of data augmentation. Most of the results are quite similar to those in Figure 5.3, although note that the fractions of missing information for lenroll and private are much lower than before.

When the fraction of missing information is high, more than the recommended three to five completed data sets may be necessary to get stable estimates. How many might that be? Multiple imputation with an infinite number of data sets is fully efficient (like ML), but MI with a finite number of data sets does not achieve full efficiency. Rubin (1987) showed that the relative efficiency of an estimate based on M data sets compared with an estimate based on an infinite number of data sets is given by $(1 + \gamma/M)^{-1}$, where γ is the fraction of missing information. This implies that with five data sets and 50% missing information, the efficiency of the estimation procedure is 91%. With 10 data sets, the efficiency goes up to 95%. Equivalently, using only five data sets would give us standard errors that are 5% larger than when an infinite number of data sets is used. Ten data sets would yield standard errors that are 2.5% larger than an infinite number of data sets. The bottom line is that even with 50% missing information, five data sets do a pretty good job. Doubling the number of data sets cuts the excess standard error in half, but the excess is small to begin with.

Before leaving the regression example, let us compare the MI results in Figure 5.4 with the ML results in Table 4.6. The coefficient estimates are quite similar, as are the standard errors and t statistics. Certainly the same conclusions would be reached from the two analyses.

6. MULTIPLE IMPUTATION: COMPLICATIONS

Interactions and Nonlinearities in MI

Although the methods we have just described are very good for estimating the main effects of the variables with missing data, they may not be so good for estimating interaction effects. Suppose, for example, we suspect that the effect of SAT scores (CSAT) on graduation rate (GRADRAT) is different for public and private colleges. One way to test this hypothesis (Method 1) would be to take the previously imputed data, create a new variable that is the product of CSAT

TABLE 6.1
Regressions With Interaction Terms—Three Methods

Variable	Method 1		Method 2		Method 3	
	Coefficient	p Value	Coefficient	p Value	Coefficient	p Value
INTERCEPT	−39.142	.000	−48.046	.000	−50.2	.000
CSAT	0.073	.000	0.085	.000	0.085	.000
LENROLL	2.383	.000	1.932	.001	1.950	.013
STUFAC	−0.175	.205	−0.204	.083	−0.152	.091
PRIVATE	20.870	.023	35.128	.001	36.118	.002
RMBRD	2.134	.002	2.448	.000	2.641	.003
PRIVCSAT	−0.008	.388	−0.024	.022	−0.024	.024

and PRIVATE, and include this product term in the regression equation along with the other variables already in the model. The leftmost panel of Table 6.1 (Method 1) shows the results of doing this. The variable PRIVCSAT is the product of CSAT and PRIVATE. With a p value of .39, the interaction is far from statistically significant, so we conclude that the effect of CSAT does not vary between public and private institutions.

The problem with this approach is that although the multivariate normal model is good at imputing values that reproduce the linear relationships among variables, it does not model any higher-order moments. Consequently, the imputed values display no evidence of interaction unless special techniques are implemented. In this example, where one of the two variables in the interaction is a dichotomy (PRIVATE), the most natural solution (Method 2) is to do separate chains of data augmentation for private colleges and for public colleges. This allows the relationship between CSAT and GRADRAT to differ across the two groups and allows the imputed values to reflect that fact. Once the separate imputations are completed, the data sets are recombined into a single data set, the product variable is created, and the regression is run with the product variable. Results in the middle panel of Table 6.1 show that the interaction between PRIVATE and CSAT is significant at the .02 level. More specifically, we find that the positive effect of CSAT on graduation rates is smaller in private colleges than in public colleges.

A third approach (Method 3) is to create the product variable for all cases with observed values of CSAT and PRIVATE *before* imputation, then impute the product variable just like any other variable with missing data, and, finally, using the imputed data, estimate the regression model that includes the product variable. This method is less appealing than Method 2 because the product variable typically will have a distribution that is far from normal, yet normality is assumed in the imputation process. Nevertheless, as seen in the right-hand panel of Table 6.1, the results from Method 3 are very close to those obtained with Method 2 and certainly much closer than those of Method 1.

The results for Method 3 are reassuring because Method 2 is not feasible when both variables in the interaction are measured on quantitative scales. Thus, if we wish to estimate a model with the interaction of CSAT and RMBRD, we need to create a product variable for the 476 cases that have data on both these variables. For the remaining 826 cases, we must impute the product term as part of the data augmentation process. This method (or Method 2 when possible) should be used whenever the goal is to estimate a model with nonlinear relationships that involves variables with missing data. For example, if we want to estimate a model with both RMBRD and RMBRD squared, the squared term should be imputed as part of the data augmentation. This requirement puts some burden on the imputer to anticipate the desired functional form before beginning the imputation. It also means that we must be cautious about estimating nonlinear models from data that have been imputed by others using strictly linear models. Of course, if the percentage of missing data on a given variable is small, we may be able to get by with imputing a variable in its original form and then constructing a nonlinear transformation later. Certainly for the variable STUFAC (student/faculty ratio), with only two cases missing out of 1,302, it would be quite acceptable to put STUFAC squared in a regression model after simply squaring the two imputed values rather than imputing the squared values.

Compatibility of the Imputation Model and the Analysis Model

The problem of interactions illustrates a more general issue in multiple imputation. Ideally, the model used for imputation should agree with the model used in analysis, and both should correctly represent the data. The basic formula (Equation 5.1) for computing standard errors depends on this compatibility and correctness.

What happens when the imputation and analysis models differ? That depends on the nature of the difference and which model is correct (Schafer, 1997). Of particular interest are cases in which one model is a special case of the other. For example, the imputation model may allow for interactions, but the analysis model may not, or the analysis model may allow for interactions, but the imputation model may not. In either case, if the additional restrictions imposed by the simpler model are correct, then the procedures we have discussed for inference under multiple imputation will be valid. However, if the additional restrictions are not correct, inferences that use the standard methods may not be valid.

Methods that are less sensitive to model choice have been proposed for estimating standard errors under multiple imputation (Wang & Robins, 1998; Robins & Wang, 2000). Specifically, these methods give valid standard error estimates when the imputation and analysis models are incompatible and when both models are incorrect. Nevertheless, incorrect models at either stage still may give biased parameter estimates, and the alternative methods require specialized software that is not yet readily available.

Role of the Dependent Variable in Imputation

Because GRADRAT was one of the variables included in the data augmentation process, the dependent variable was implicitly used to impute missing values on the independent variables. Is this legitimate? Does it not tend to produce spuriously large regression coefficients? The answer is that not only is this OK, it is *essential* for getting unbiased estimates of the regression coefficients. With deterministic imputation, using the dependent variable to impute the missing values of the independent variables can, indeed, produce spuriously large regression coefficients, but the introduction of a random component into the imputation process counterbalances this tendency and gives us approximately unbiased estimates. In fact, leaving the dependent variable out of the imputation process tends to produce regression coefficients that are spuriously small, at least for those variables that have missing data (Landerman, Land, & Pieper, 1997). In the college example, if GRADRAT is not used in the imputations, the coefficients for CSAT and RMBRD, both with large fractions of missing data, are reduced by about 25% and 20%, respectively. At the same time, the coefficient for LENROLL, which only had five missing values, is 65% larger.

Of course, including GRADRAT in the data augmentation process also means that any missing values of GRADRAT also were imputed. Some authors have recommended against imputing missing data on the dependent variable (Cohen & Cohen, 1985). To follow this advice, we would have to delete any cases with missing data on the dependent variable before beginning the imputation. There is a valid rationale for this recommendation, but it applies only in special cases. If there are missing data on the dependent variable but *not* on any of the independent variables, maximum likelihood estimation of a regression model (whether linear or nonlinear) does not use any information from cases with missing data. Because ML is optimal, there is nothing to gain from imputing the missing cases under multiple imputation. In fact, although such imputation would not lead to any bias, the standard errors would be larger. However, the situation changes when there is also missing data on the independent variables. Then cases with missing values on the dependent variables do have some information to contribute to the estimation of the regression coefficients, although probably not a great deal. The upshot is that in the typical case with missing values on both dependent and independent variables, the cases with missing values on the dependent variable should not be deleted.

Using Additional Variables in the Imputation Process

As already noted, the set of variables used in data augmentation certainly should include all variables that will be used in the planned analysis. In the college example, we also included one additional variable, ACT (mean ACT scores), because of its high correlation with CSAT, a variable that had substantial missing data. The goal was to improve the imputations of CSAT to get more reliable estimates of its regression coefficient. We might have done even better had we included still other variables that were correlated with CSAT.

A somewhat simpler example illustrates the benefits of additional predictor variables. Suppose we want to estimate the mean CSAT score across the 1,302 colleges. As we know, data are missing on CSAT for 523 cases. If we calculate the mean for the other 779 cases with values on CSAT, we get the results in the first line of Table 6.2. The

TABLE 6.2
Means (and Standard Errors) of CSAT With Different Variables
Used in Imputation

Variables Used in Imputing	Mean	Standard Error	% Missing Information
None	967.98	4.43	40.1[a]
ACT	956.87	3.84	26.5
ACT, PCT25	959.48	3.60	13.3
ACT, PCT25, GRADRAT	958.04	3.58	11.3

[a] Actual percentage of missing data.

next line shows the estimated mean (with standard error) using multiple imputation and the ACT variable. The mean has decreased by 9 points, whereas the standard error has decreased by 13%. Although ACT has a correlation of about 0.90 with CSAT, its usefulness as a predictor variable is somewhat marred by the fact that values are observed on ACT for only 226 of the 523 cases missing on CSAT. If we add an additional variable, PCT25 (the percentage of students in the top 25% of their class), we get an additional reduction in standard error. PCT25 has a correlation of about 0.80 with CSAT and is available for an additional 240 cases that have missing data on both CSAT and ACT.

The last line of Table 6.2 adds in GRADRAT, which has a correlation of about 0.60 with CSAT, but is only available for 17 cases not already covered by PCT25 or ACT. Not surprisingly, the decline in the standard error is quite small. When I tried to introduce all the other variables in the regression model in Figure 5.4, the standard error actually got larger. This is likely due to the fact that the other variables have much lower correlations with CSAT, yet additional variability is introduced because of the need to estimate their regression coefficients for predicting CSAT. As in other forecasting problems, imputations may get worse when poor predictors are added to the model.

Other Parametric Approaches to Multiple Imputation

As we have seen, multiple imputation under the multivariate normal model is reasonably straightforward under a wide variety of data types and missing data patterns. As a routine method for handling missing data, it is probably the best that is currently available. There are, however, several alternative approaches that may be preferable in some circumstances.

One of the most obvious limitations of the multivariate normal model is that it is designed only to impute missing values for quantitative variables. As we have seen, categorical variables can be accommodated by using some ad hoc fixups. However, sometimes you may want to do better. For situations in which *all* variables in the imputation process are categorical, a more attractive model is the unrestricted multinomial model (which has a parameter for every cell in the contingency table) or a log-linear model that allows restrictions on the multinomial parameters. In Chapter 4, we discussed ML estimation of these models. Schafer (1997) showed how these models also can be used as the basis for data augmentation to produce multiple imputations and he developed a freeware program called CAT to implement the method (http://www.stat.psu.edu/~jls/).

Another Schafer program (MIX) uses data augmentation to generate imputations when the data consist of a mixture of categorical and quantitative variables. This method presumes that the categorical variables have a multinomial distribution, possibly with log-linear restrictions on the parameters. Within each cell of the contingency table created by the categorical variables, the quantitative variables are assumed to have a multivariate normal distribution. The means of these variables are allowed to vary across cells, but the covariance matrix is assumed to be constant.

At this writing, both CAT and MIX are available only as libraries to the S-PLUS statistical package, although stand-alone versions are promised. In both cases, the underlying models potentially have many more parameters than the multivariate normal model. As a result, effective use of these methods typically requires more knowledge and input from the person performing the imputation, together with larger sample sizes to achieve stable estimates.

If data are missing for a single categorical variable, multiple imputation under a logistic (logit) regression model is reasonably straightforward (Rubin, 1987). Suppose data are missing on marital status, coded into five categories, and there are several potential predictor variables, both continuous and categorical. For the purposes of imputation, we estimate a multinomial logit model for marital status as a function of the predictors, using cases with complete data. This produces a set of coefficient estimates $\hat{\beta}$ and an estimate of the covariance matrix $\widehat{V}(\hat{\beta})$. To allow for variability in the parameter estimates, we take a random draw from a normal distribution with a mean of $\hat{\beta}$ and a covariance matrix $\widehat{V}(\hat{\beta})$. (Schafer [1997] gave practical suggestions on how to do this efficiently.) For each case with missing data, the drawn coefficient values and the observed covariate values are substituted into the multinomial logit model to generate predicted probabilities of falling into the five marital status categories. Based on these predicted probabilities, we randomly draw one of the marital status categories as the final imputed value.[12] The whole process is repeated multiple times to generate multiple completed data sets. Of course, a binary variable would be just a special case of this method. This approach also can be used with a variety of other parametric models, including Poisson regression and parametric failure-time regressions.

Nonparametric and Partially Parametric Methods

Many methods have been proposed for doing multiple imputation under less stringent assumptions than the fully parametric methods we have just considered. In this section, I will consider a few representative approaches, but keep in mind that each of these approaches has many different variations. All these methods are most naturally applied when there are missing data on only a single variable, although they often can be generalized without difficulty to multiple variables when data are missing in a monotone pattern (described in Chapter 4). See Rubin (1987) for details on monotone generalizations. These methods can sometimes be used when the missing data do *not* follow a monotone pattern, but in such settings they typically lack solid theoretical justification.

When choosing between parametric and nonparametric methods, there is the usual trade-off between bias and sampling variability. Parametric methods tend to have less sampling variability, but they may give biased estimates if the parametric model is not a good approximation to the phenomenon of interest. Nonparametric methods may be less prone to bias under a variety of situations, but the estimates often have more sampling variability.

Hot Deck Methods

The best-known approach to nonparametric imputation is the "hot deck" method, which is frequently used by the U.S. Census Bureau to produce imputed values for public-use data sets. The basic idea is that we want to impute missing values for a particular variable Y, which may be either quantitative or categorical. We find a set of categorical X variables (with no missing data) that are associated with Y. We form a contingency table based on the X variables. If there are cases with missing Y values within a particular cell of the contingency table, we take one or more of the nonmissing cases in the same cell and use their Y values to impute the missing Y values.

Obviously there are a lot of complications that may arise. The critical question is how do you choose which "donor" values to assign to the cases with missing values? Clearly the choice of donor cases should be randomized somehow to avoid bias. This leads naturally to multiple imputation because any randomized method can be applied more than once to produce different imputed values. The trick is to do the randomization in such a way that all the natural variability is preserved. To accomplish this, Rubin proposed a method he coined the approximate Bayesian bootstrap (Rubin, 1987; Rubin & Schenker, 1991). Here is how it is done. Suppose that in a particular cell of the contingency table there are n_1 cases with complete data on Y and n_0 cases with missing data on Y. Follow these steps:

1. From the set of n_1 cases with complete data, take a random sample (with replacement) of n_1 cases.
2. From this sample, take a random sample (with replacement) of n_0 cases.
3. Assign the n_0 observed values of Y to the n_0 cases with missing data on Y.
4. Repeat steps 1 to 3 for every cell in the contingency table.

These four steps produce one completed data set when applied to all cells of the contingency table. For multiple imputation, the whole process is repeated multiple times. After the desired analysis is performed on each data set, the results are combined using the same formulas we used for multivariate normal imputations.

Although it might seem that we could skip step 1 and directly choose n_0 donor cases from among the n_1 cases with complete data, this does not produce sufficient variability for estimating standard errors. Additional variability comes from the fact that sampling in step 2 is with replacement.

Predictive Mean Matching

A major attraction of hot deck imputation is that the imputed values are all actual observed values. Consequently, there are no "impossible" or out-of-range values, and the shape of the distribution tends to be preserved. A disadvantage is that the predictor variables all must be categorical (or treated as such), which imposes serious limitations on the number of possible predictor variables. To remove this limitation, Little (1988) proposed a partially parametric method called *predictive mean matching*. Like the multivariate normal parametric method, this approach begins by regressing Y, the variable to be imputed, on a set of predictors for cases with complete data. This regression is then used to generate predicted values for both the missing and the nonmissing cases. Then, for each case with missing data, we find a set of cases with complete data that have predicted values of Y that are "close" to the predicted value for the case with missing data. From this set of cases, we randomly choose one case whose Y value is donated to the missing case.

For a single Y variable, it is straightforward to define closeness as the absolute difference between predicted values. However, then we must decide how many of the close predicted values to include in the donor pool for each missing case or, equivalently, what should be the cutoff point in closeness for forming the set of possible donor values? If a small donor pool is chosen, there will be more sampling variability in the estimates. On the other hand, too large a donor pool can lead to possible bias because many donors may be unlike the recipients. To deal with this ambiguity, Schenker and Taylor (1996) developed an "adaptive method" that varies the size of the donor pool for each missing case based on the "density" of complete cases with close predicted values. They found that their method did somewhat better than methods with fixed size donor pools of either 3 or 10 closest cases. However, the differences among the three methods were sufficiently small that the adaptive method hardly seems worth the extra computational cost.

In doing predictive mean matching, it is also important to adjust for the fact that the regression coefficients are only estimates of the true coefficients. As in the parametric case, this can be accomplished by randomly drawing a new set of regression parameters from their posterior distribution before calculating predicted values for each imputed data set. Here is how to do it:

1. Regress Y on X (a vector of covariates) for the n_1 cases with no missing data on Y, producing regression coefficients b (a $k \times 1$ vector) and residual variance estimate s^2.

2. Make a random draw from the posterior distribution of the residual variance (assuming a noninformative prior). This is accomplished by calculating $(n_1 - k) s^2/\chi^2$, where χ^2 represents a random draw from a chi-square distribution with $n_1 - k$ degrees of freedom. Let $s_{[1]}^2$ be the first such random draw.

3. Make a random draw from the posterior distribution of the regression coefficients. This is accomplished by drawing from a multivariate normal distribution with mean b and covariance matrix $s_{[1]}^2 (\mathbf{X'X})^{-1}$, where $\mathbf{X}$ is an $n_1 \times k$ matrix of X values. Let $b_{[1]}$ be the first such random draw. See Schafer (1997) for practical suggestions on how to do this.

For each new set of regression parameters, predicted values are generated for all cases. Then, for each case with missing data on Y, we form a donor pool based on the predicted values and randomly choose one of the observed values of Y from the donor pool. This approach to predictive mean matching can be generalized to more than one Y variable with missing data, although the computations may become rather complex (Little, 1988).

Sampling on Empirical Residuals

In the data augmentation method, residual values are sampled from a standard normal distribution and then added to the predicted regression values to get the final imputed values. We can modify this method to be less dependent on parametric assumptions by making random draws from the actual set of residuals produced by the linear regression. This can yield imputed values whose distribution is more like that of the observed variable (Rubin, 1987), although it is still possible to get imputed values that are outside the permissible range.

As with other approaches to multiple imputation, there are some important subtleties involved in doing this properly. As before, let Y be the variable with missing data to be imputed for n_0 cases, with observed data on n_1 cases. Let X be a $k \times 1$ vector of variables (including a constant) with no missing data on the n_1 cases. We begin by performing the preceding three steps to obtain the linear regression of

Y on X and generate random draws from the posterior distribution of the parameters. Then we add the following steps:

4. Based on the regression estimates in step 1, calculate standardized residuals for the cases with no missing data:

$$e_i = (y_i - bx_i)/\sqrt{s^2(1 - k/n_1)}$$

5. Draw a simple random sample (with replacement) of n_0 values from the n_1 residuals calculated in step 4.
6. For the n_0 cases with missing data, calculate imputed values of Y as

$$y_i = b_{[1]}x_i + s_{[1]}e_i,$$

where e_i represents the residuals drawn in step 5, and $b_{[1]}$ and $s_{[1]}$ are the first random draws from the posterior distribution of the parameters.

These six steps produce one completed set of data. To get additional data sets, simply repeat steps 2 through 6 (except for step 4, which should not be repeated).

As Rubin (1987) explained, this methodology can be readily extended to data sets with a monotonic missing pattern on several variables. Each variable is imputed using as predictors all variables that are observed when it is missing. The empirical residual method also can be modified to allow for heteroscedasticity in the imputed values (Schenker & Taylor, 1996). For each case to be imputed, the pool of residuals is restricted to those observed cases that have predicted values of Y that are close to the predicted value for the case with missing data.

Example

Let us try the partially parametric methods on a subset of the college data. TUITION is fully observed for 1,272 colleges. (For simplicity, we shall exclude the 30 cases with missing data on this variable.) Of these 1,272 colleges, only 796 report BOARD, the annual average cost of board at each college. Using TUITION as a predictor, our goal is to impute the missing values of BOARD for the other 476 colleges, and estimate the mean of BOARD for all 1,272 colleges.

First, we apply the methods we have used before. For the 796 colleges with complete data (listwise deletion), the average BOARD is $2,060 with a standard error of 23.4. Applying the EM algorithm to

TUITION and BOARD, we get a mean BOARD of 2,032 (but no standard error). The EM estimate of the correlation between BOARD and TUITION was 0.555. Multiple imputation under the multivariate normal model using data augmentation gave a mean BOARD of 2,040 with an estimated standard error of 21.2.

Because BOARD is highly skewed to the right, there is reason to suspect that the multivariate normal model may not be appropriate. Quite a few of the values imputed by data augmentation were less than the minimum observed value of 531, and one imputed value was negative. Perhaps we can do better by sampling on the empirical residuals. For the 796 cases with data on both TUITION and BOARD, the ordinary least-squares (OLS) regression of BOARD on TUITION was

$$BOARD = 1,497.4 + 67.65 * TUITION/1,000$$

with a root mean squared error (rmse) estimated at 542.6. Standardized residuals from this regression were calculated for the 796 cases.

The estimated regression parameters were used to make five random draws from the posterior distribution of the parameters as in steps 2 and 3 (assuming a noninformative prior). The drawn values were

Intercept	Slope	rmse
1536.40	66.6509	531.990
1503.65	71.5916	552.708
1501.61	66.9756	554.800
1486.84	66.9850	548.400
1504.23	61.2308	534.895

To create the first completed data set, 476 residual values were randomly drawn with replacement from among the 796 cases. These standardized residuals were assigned arbitrarily to the 476 cases with missing data on BOARD. Letting E be the assigned residual for a given case, the imputed values for BOARD were generated as

$$BOARD = 1,536.40 + 66.6509 * TUITION/1,000 + 531.990 * E.$$

This process was repeated for the four remaining data sets, with new sampling on the residuals and new values of the regression parameters at each step.

Once the five data sets were produced, the mean and standard error were computed for each data set, and the results were combined using formula 5.1 for the standard error. The final estimate for the mean of BOARD was 2,035 with an estimated standard error of 20.4, which is quite close to multiple imputation based on a normal distribution.

Now let us try predictive mean matching. Based on the coefficients from the OLS regression of BOARD on TUITION, I generated five new random draws from the posterior distribution of the regression parameters:

Intercept	Slope	rmse
1465.89	67.8732	557.531
1548.98	64.5723	539.952
1428.82	67.3901	512.381
1469.34	67.3750	550.945
1517.92	66.1926	534.804

For the first set of parameter values, I generated predicted values of BOARD for all cases, both observed and missing. For each case with missing data on BOARD, I found the five observed cases whose predicted values were closest to the predicted value for the case with missing data. I randomly chose one of those five cases and assigned its *observed* value of BOARD as the imputed value for the missing case. This process was repeated for each of the five sets of parameter values to produce five complete data sets. (It is just coincidence that the number of data sets is the same as the number of observed cases matched to each missing case.) The mean and standard error were then computed for each data set and the results were combined in the usual way. The combined mean of BOARD was 2,028 with an estimated standard error of 23.0.

All four imputation methods produced similar estimates of the means and all were noticeably lower than the mean based on list-wise deletion. Schenker and Taylor (1996) suggested that although parametric and partially parametric imputation methods tend to yield quite similar estimates of mean structures (including regression coefficients), they may produce more divergent results for the marginal distribution of the imputed variables. Their simulations indicated that for applications where the marginal distribution is of major interest, partially parametric models have a distinct advantage. This was especially true when the regressions used to generate predicted values were misspecified in various ways.

Sequential Generalized Regression Models

One of the attractions of data augmentation is that, unlike the non-parametric and semiparametric methods just discussed, it easily can handle data sets with a substantial number of variables with missing data. Unfortunately, this method requires specifying a multivariate distribution for all the variables, and that is not an easy thing to do when the variables are of many different types, for example, continuous, binary, and count data. Another approach has been proposed for handling missing data in large, complex data sets with several different variable types. Instead of fitting a single comprehensive model (e.g., the multivariate normal), a separate regression model is specified for each variable that has any missing data. For each dependent variable, the regression model is chosen to reflect the type of data. The method involves cycling through several regression models, imputing missing values at each step.

Although this approach is very appealing, it does not yet have as strong a theoretical justification as the other methods we have considered. At this writing, the only detailed accounts are the unpublished reports of Brand (1999), Van Buuren and Oudshoorn (1999), and Raghunathan, Lepkowski, Van Hoewyk, and Solenberger (1999). In the Raghunathan et al. version of this method, the available models include normal linear regression, binary logistic regression, multinomial logit, and Poisson regression. The regression models are estimated in a particular order, beginning with the dependent variable with the least missing data and proceeding to the dependent variable with the most missing data. Let us denote these variables by Y_1 through Y_k and let X denote the set of variables with no missing data.

The first "round" of estimation proceeds as follows. Regress Y_1 on X and generate imputed values using a method similar to that described previously for the multinomial logit model in the section "Other Parametric Approaches to Multiple Imputation." Bounds and restrictions may be placed on the imputed values. Then regress Y_2 on X and Y_1, including the imputed values of Y_1, and generate imputed values for Y_2. Then regress Y_3 on X, Y_1, and Y_2 (including imputed values on both Ys). Continue until all the regressions have been estimated. The second and subsequent rounds repeat this process, except that now each variable is regressed on *all* other variables using any imputed values from previous steps. The process continues for a prespecified number of rounds or until stable imputed values occur. A SAS macro for accomplishing these tasks is available at http://www.isr.umich.edu/src/smp/ive.

For their version of the method, Van Buuren and Oudshoorn coined the name MICE (for multiple imputation by chained equations), and they developed S-PLUS functions to implement it (available at http://www.multiple-imputation.com/). The major differences between their approach and that of Raghunathan et al. is that MICE does not include Poisson regression, but does allow more options (both parametric and partially parametric) in the methods for random draws of imputed values.

Linear Hypothesis Tests and Likelihood Ratio Tests

To this point, our approach to statistical inference with multiple imputation has been very simple. For a given parameter, the standard error of the estimate is calculated using formula 5.1. This standard error is then plugged into conventional formulas based on the normal approximation to produce a confidence interval or a t statistic for some hypothesis of interest. Sometimes this is not enough. Often we want to test hypotheses about sets of parameters, for example, that two parameters are equal to each other or that several parameters are all equal to zero. These sorts of hypotheses are particularly relevant when we estimate several coefficients for a set of dummy variables. In addition, there is often a need to compute likelihood ratio statistics by comparing one model with another, simpler model. Accomplishing these tasks is not so straightforward when doing multiple imputation. Schafer (1997) described three different approaches, none of which is totally satisfactory. I will briefly describe them here and we will look at an example in the next section.

Wald Tests Using Combined Covariance Matrices

When there are no missing data, a common approach to multiple parameter inference is to compute Wald chi-square statistics based on the parameter estimates and their estimated covariance matrix. Here is a review, which, unfortunately, requires matrix algebra. Suppose we want to estimate a $p \times 1$ parameter vector β. We have estimates $\hat{\beta}$ and estimated covariance matrix C. We want to test a linear hypothesis expressed as $L\beta = c$, where L is an $r \times p$ matrix of constants and c is an $r \times 1$ vector of constants. For example, if we want to test the hypothesis that the first two elements of $\boldsymbol{\beta}$ are equal to each other, we need $\mathbf{L} = [1 \quad -1 \quad 0 \quad 0 \quad 0 \quad \cdots \quad 0]$ and $\mathbf{c} = 0$. The Wald test is computed as

$$W = (\mathbf{L}\hat{\boldsymbol{\beta}} - \mathbf{c})'[\mathbf{LCL}']^{-1}(\mathbf{L}\hat{\boldsymbol{\beta}} - \mathbf{c}), \qquad [6.1]$$

which has an approximate chi-square distribution with r degrees of freedom under the null hypothesis.[13]

Now we generalize this method to the multiple imputation setting. Instead of $\hat{\boldsymbol{\beta}}$, we can use $\bar{\boldsymbol{\beta}}$, the mean of the estimates across several completed data sets, that is,

$$\bar{\boldsymbol{\beta}} = \frac{1}{M-1}\sum_k \hat{\boldsymbol{\beta}}_k.$$

Next we need an estimate of the covariance matrix that combines the within-sample variability and the between-sample variability. Let $\mathbf{C}_k$ be the estimated covariance matrix for the parameters in data set k and let $\overline{\mathbf{C}}$ be the average of those matrices across the M data sets. The between-sample variability is defined as

$$\mathbf{B} = \frac{1}{M-1}\sum_k (\hat{\boldsymbol{\beta}}_k - \bar{\boldsymbol{\beta}})(\hat{\boldsymbol{\beta}}_k - \bar{\boldsymbol{\beta}})'.$$

The combined estimate of the covariance matrix is then

$$\widetilde{\mathbf{C}} = \overline{\mathbf{C}} + (1 + 1/M)\mathbf{B},$$

which is just a multivariate generalization of formula 5.1 without the square root. We get our test statistic by formula 6.1 with $\bar{\boldsymbol{\beta}}$ and $\widetilde{\mathbf{C}}$ substituted for $\hat{\boldsymbol{\beta}}$ and $\mathbf{C}$.

Unfortunately, this does not work well in the typical case where M is 5 or less. In such cases, $\mathbf{B}$ is a rather unstable estimate of the between-sample covariance, and the resulting distribution of W is not chi-square. Schafer (1997) gave a more stable estimator for the covariance matrix, but this required the unreasonable assumption that the fraction of missing information is the same for all the elements of $\hat{\boldsymbol{\beta}}$. Nevertheless, some simulations show that this alternate method works well even when the assumption is violated. This method has been incorporated into the SAS procedure MIANALYZE.

Likelihood Ratio Tests

If the model of interest is estimated by maximum likelihood and there are no missing data, multiparameter tests are often performed by computing likelihood ratio chi-squares. The procedure is quite simple. Let l_0 be the log-likelihood for a model that imposes the hypothesis and let l_1 be the log-likelihood for a model that relaxes the hypothesis. The likelihood ratio statistic is just $L = 2(l_1 - l_0)$.

As before, our goal is to generalize this to multiple imputation. The first step is to perform the desired likelihood ratio test in each of the M completed data sets. Let $\overline{L}$ be the mean of the likelihood ratio chi-squares computed across those M data sets. That is the easy part. Now comes the hard part. To get those chi-squares, it was necessary to estimate two models in each data set, one with the hypothesis imposed and one with the hypothesis relaxed. Let $\bar{\boldsymbol{\beta}}_0$ be the mean of the M parameter estimates when the hypothesis is imposed and let $\bar{\boldsymbol{\beta}}_1$ be the mean of the parameter estimates when the hypothesis is relaxed. In each data set, we then compute the log-likelihood for a model with parameter values forced to be $\bar{\boldsymbol{\beta}}_0$ and again for a model with parameters set at $\bar{\boldsymbol{\beta}}_1$. (This obviously requires that the software be able to calculate and report log-likelihoods for user-specified parameter values.) Based on these two log-likelihoods, a likelihood ratio chi-square is computed in each data set. Let $\widetilde{L}$ be the mean of these chi-square statistics across the M samples.

The final test statistic is then $\widetilde{L}/(r + (\frac{M+1}{M-1})(\overline{L} - \widetilde{L}))$, where r is the number of restrictions imposed by the hypothesis. Under the null hypothesis, this statistic has approximately an F distribution with numerator degrees of freedom equal to r. The denominator degrees of freedom (d.d.f) is somewhat awkward to calculate. Let $t = r(M-1)$ and let

$$q = \left(\frac{M+1}{M-1}\right)\left(\frac{\overline{L} - \widetilde{L}}{r}\right).$$

If $t > 4$, the d.d.f. $= 4 + (t - 4)[1 + (1 - 2/t)/q]^2$. If $t \leq 4$, the d.d.f. $= t(1 + 1/r)(1 + 1/q)^2/2$.

Combining Chi-Square Statistics

Both the Wald test and the likelihood ratio test lack the appealing simplicity of the single-parameter methods used earlier. In particular, they require that the analysis software have specialized options and output, something we have generally tried to avoid. I now discuss a third method that is easy to compute from standard output, but may not be as accurate as the other two methods (Li, Meng, Raghunathan, & Rubin, 1991). All that is needed is the conventional chi-square statistic (either Wald or likelihood ratio) calculated in each of the M completed data sets, and the associated degrees of freedom.

Let d_k^2 be a chi-square statistic with r degrees of freedom calculated in data set k. Let $\bar{d}^2$ be the mean of these statistics over the M data sets and let s_d^2 be the sample variance of the *square roots* of the chi-square statistics over the M data sets, that is,

$$s_d^2 = \frac{1}{M-1} \sum_k (d_k - \bar{d})^2.$$

The proposed test statistic is

$$D = \frac{\bar{d}^2/r - (1 - 1/M)s_d^2}{1 + (1 + 1/M)s_d^2}.$$

Under the null hypothesis, this statistic has approximately an F distribution with r as the numerator degrees of freedom. The denominator degrees of freedom is approximated by

$$\left(\frac{M-1}{r^{3/M}}\right)\left(1 + \frac{M}{(M+1/M)s_d^2}\right)^2.$$

I have written a SAS macro (COMBCHI) to perform these computations and compute a p value. It is available on my Web site (http://www.ssc.upenn.edu/~allison). To use it, all you need to do is enter several chi-square values and the degrees of freedom. The macro returns a p value.

MI Example 2

Let us consider another detailed empirical example that illustrates some of the techniques discussed in this chapter. The data set consists of 2,992 respondents to the 1994 General Social Survey (Davis & Smith, 1997). Our dependent variable is SPANKING, a response to the question, "Do you strongly agree, agree, disagree, or strongly disagree that it is sometimes necessary to discipline a child with a good, hard spanking?" As the question itself indicates, there were four possible ordered responses, coded as integers 1 through 4. By design, this question was part of a module that was administered only to a random two-thirds of the sample. Thus, there were 1,015 cases that were missing completely at random. In addition, another 27 respondents were missing with responses coded "don't know" or "no answer."

Our goal is to estimate an ordered logistic (cumulative logit) model (McCullagh, 1980) in which SPANKING is predicted by the following variables:

AGE	Respondent's age in years, ranging from 18 to 89. Missing 6 cases.
EDUC	Number of years of schooling. Missing 7 cases.
INCOME	Household income, coded as the midpoint of 21 interval categories, in thousands of dollars. Missing 356 cases.
FEMALE	1 = female; 0 = male.
BLACK	1 = black; 0 = white, other.
MARITAL	Five categories of marital status. Missing 1 case.
REGION	Nine categories of region.
NOCHILD	1 = no children; otherwise 0. Missing 9 cases.

One additional variable, NODOUBT, requires further explanation. Respondents were asked about their beliefs in God. There were six response categories ranging from "I don't believe in God" to "I know God really exists and I have no doubts about it." The latter statement was the modal response with 62% of the respondents. However, like the spanking question, this question was part of a module that was only asked of a random subset of 1,386 respondents. So there were 1,606 cases missing by design. Another 60 cases were treated as missing because they said "don't know" or "no answer." As used here, the variable was coded 1 if the respondent had "no doubts"; otherwise it was coded 0.

Most of the missing data are on three variables, SPANKING, NODOUBT, and INCOME. There were five major missing data patterns in the sample, accounting for 96% of respondents:

771 cases   No missing data on any variables
927 cases   Missing NODOUBT only

421 cases	Missing SPANKING only
80 cases	Missing INCOME only
509 cases	Missing SPANKING and NODOUBT
160 cases	Missing NODOUBT and INCOME

As usual, the simplest approach to data analysis is listwise deletion, which uses only 26% of the original sample. To specify the
model, I created dummy variables for three marital status categories:
NEVMAR (for never married), DIVSEP (for divorced or separated),
and WIDOW (for widowed), with married as the reference category.
Three dummy variables were created for region (with West as the
omitted category).[14] Results (produced by PROC LOGISTIC in SAS)
are shown in the first column of Table 6.3. Blacks, older respondents,
and respondents with "no doubts" about God are more likely to favor
spanking. Women and more educated respondents are more likely
to oppose it. There are also major regional differences: respondents
from the South were more favorable toward spanking and those from
the Northeast were more opposed. On the other hand, there is no
evidence for any effect of income, marital status, or having children.

Because 84% of the observations with missing data are missing by design (and hence completely at random), listwise deletion
should produce approximately unbiased estimates. However, the loss
of nearly three-quarters of the sample is a big price to pay—one
that is avoidable with multiple imputation. To implement MI, I first
used the data augmentation method under the multivariate normal
model described in Chapter 5. Before beginning the process, the single case with missing data on marital status was deleted to avoid
having to impute a multicategory variable. A reasonable argument
could be made for also deleting the 1,042 cases that were missing the
SPANKING variable, because cases that are missing on the dependent variable contain little information about regression coefficients.
However, there is no harm in including them and potentially some
benefit, so I kept them in. All 13 variables in the model were included
in the imputation process without any normalizing transformations.

The imputed values for all the dummy variables were rounded to
0 or 1. The imputed values for SPANKING were rounded to the
integers 1 through 4. Age and income had some imputed values that
were out of the valid range, and these were recoded to the upper
or lower bounds. The cumulative logit model was then estimated for

TABLE 6.3
Coefficient Estimates (and Standard Errors)
for Cumulative Logit Models Predicting SPANKING

Variable	Listwise Deletion	Normal Data Augmentation	Sequential Regression	Seq. Regression (Number Missing on SPANKING)
FEMALE	−0.355 (0.141)*	−0.481 (0.089)***	−0.449 (0.098)***	−0.489 (0.094)***
BLACK	0.565 (0.218)**	0.756 (0.117)***	0.693 (0.119)***	0.685 (0.135)***
INCOME	−0.0036 (0.0033)	−0.0052 (0.0020)*	−0.0042 (0.0027)	−0.0047 (0.0022)*
EDUC	−0.055 (0.027)*	−0.061 (0.016)***	−0.073 (0.019)**	−0.068 (0.016)***
NODOUBT	0.454 (0.147)**	0.465 (0.120)**	0.455 (0.156)*	0.438 (0.121)**
NOCHILD	−0.205 (0.199)	−0.109 (0.112)	−0.141 (0.164)	−0.091 (0.123)
AGE	0.010 (0.005)*	0.0043 (0.0032)	0.0031 (0.0032)	0.0040 (0.0031)
EAST	−0.712 (0.219)**	−0.444 (0.125)***	−0.519 (0.156)**	−0.488 (0.136)***
MIDWEST	−0.122 (0.203)	−0.161 (0.136)	−0.228 (0.149)	−0.159 (0.128)
SOUTH	0.404 (0.191)**	0.323 (0.156)*	0.262 (0.129)*	0.357 (0.121)**
NEVMAR	−0.046 (0.238)	−0.075 (0.148)	−0.036 (0.173)	−0.071 (0.151)
DIVSEP	−0.191 (0.194)	−0.203 (0.150)	−0.141 (0.128)	−0.184 (0.126)
WIDOW	0.148 (0.298)	−0.244 (0.150)	−0.116 (0.177)	−0.215 (0.174)

*$p < 0.05$; **$p < 0.01$; ***$p < 0.001$.

each of the five data sets and the estimates were combined using the standard formulas.

Results are shown in the second column of Table 6.3. The basic pattern is the same, although there is now a significant effect of INCOME and a loss of significance for AGE. What is most striking is that the standard errors for all the coefficients are substantially lower than those for listwise deletion, typically by about 40%. Even the standard error for NODOUBT is 18% smaller, which is surprising given that over half the cases were missing on this variable. The smaller standard errors yield p values that are much lower for many of the variables.

The cumulative logit model imposes a constraint on the data known as the *proportional odds assumption*. In brief, this phrase means that the coefficients are assumed to be the same for any dichotomization of the dependent variable. PROC LOGISTIC reports a chi-square statistic (score test) for the null hypothesis that the proportional odds assumption is correct. However, because we are working with five data sets, we get five chi-squares, each with 26 degrees of freedom: 32.0, 31.3, 38.0, 36.4, and 35.2. Using the COMBCHI macro described earlier, these five values are combined to produce a p value of .25, suggesting that the constraint imposed by the model fits the data well. For each of the five data sets, I also calculated Wald chi-squares for the null hypothesis that all the region coefficients were zero. With 3 d.f., the values were 72.9, 81.3, 53.4, 67.7, and 67.0. The combined p value was .00002.

In the third column of Table 6.3, we see results from applying the multiple imputation method of Raghunathan et al. (1999), which relies on sequential generalized regressions. A regression model was estimated for each variable with missing data, which was taken as the dependent variable, and all other variables were predictors. These regression models then were used to generate five sets of random imputations. For EDUC and INCOME, the models were ordinary linear regression models, although upper and lower bounds were built into the imputation process. Logistic regression models were specified for NODOUBT and NOCHILD. A multinomial logit model was used for SPANKING. There were 20 rounds in the imputation process, which means that for each of the five completed data sets, the variables with missing data were sequentially imputed 20 times before using the final result.

As before, the cumulative logit model was estimated on each of the five completed data sets and the results were combined using the standard formulas. The coefficient estimates in the third column of Table 6.3 are quite similar to those for multivariate normal data augmentation. The standard errors are generally a little higher than those for data augmentation, although not nearly as high as those for listwise deletion.

Somewhat surprising is the fact that the chi-square statistics for the proportional odds assumption are nearly twice as large for sequential regression compared with those for normal data augmentation. Specifically, with 26 degrees of freedom, the values were 54.9, 59.9, 66.7, 85.4, and 59.0, each with a p value well below .001. However, when the values are combined using the COMBCHI macro, the resulting p value is .45. Why the great disparity between the individual p values and the combined value? The answer is that the large variance among the chi-squares is an indication that each one of them may be a substantial overestimate. The formula for combining them takes this into account.

What accounts for the disparity between the chi-squares for normal data augmentation and those for sequential regression? I suspect that stems from the fact that the multinomial logit model for imputing

SPANKING did not impose any ordering on that variable. As a result, the imputed values were less likely to correspond to the proportional odds assumption. When the sequential imputations were redone with a linear model for SPANKING (with rounding of imputed values to integers), the chi-squares for the proportional odds assumption were more in line with those obtained under normal data augmentation. Alternatively, I redid the sequential imputations after first deleting all missing cases on SPANKING. SPANKING was still specified as categorical, which means that it was treated as a categorical *predictor* when imputing the values of other variables. Again, the chi-squares for the proportional odds assumption were similar to those that resulted from normal data augmentation.

The last column of Table 6.3 shows the combined results with sequential regression imputation after deleting missing cases on SPANKING. Interestingly, both the coefficients and their standard errors are generally closer to those for data augmentation than to those for sequential imputation with all missing data imputed. Furthermore, there is no apparent loss of information when we delete the 1,042 cases with data missing on SPANKING.

MI for Longitudinal and Other Clustered Data

So far, we have assumed that every observation is independent of every other observation, a reasonable presumption if the data are a simple random sample from some large population. However, many data sets are likely to have some dependence among the observations. Suppose, for example, that we have a panel of individuals for whom the same variables are measured annually for five years. Many computer programs for analyzing panel data require that data be organized so that the measurements in each year are treated as separate observations. To link observations together, there also must be a variable that contains an identification number that is common to all observations from the same individual.

Thus, if we had 100 individuals observed annually for five years, we would have 500 working observations. Clearly, these observations would not be independent. If the multiple imputation methods already discussed were applied directly to these 500 observations, none of the longitudinal information would be utilized. As a result, the completed data sets could yield substantial underestimates of the longitudinal correlations, especially if there were large amounts of missing data.

Similar problems arise if the observations fall into naturally occurring clusters. Suppose we have a sample of 500 married couples, and the same battery of questions is administered to both husband and wife. If we impute missing data for either spouse, it is important to do it in a way that uses the correlation between the spouses' responses. The same is true for students in the same classroom or respondents in the same neighborhood.

One approach to these kinds of data is to do multiple imputation under a model that builds in the dependence among the observations. Schafer (1997) proposed a multivariate, linear mixed-effects model for clustered data and also developed a computer program (PAN) to do the imputation using the method of data augmentation (available on the Web at http://www.stat.psu.edu/~jls/). Although a Windows version of this program is promised, the current version runs only as a library to the S-PLUS package.

There is also a much simpler approach that works well for panel data when the number of waves is relatively small. The basic idea is to format the data so that there is only one record for each individual and with distinct variables for the measurements on the same variable at different points in time. Multiple imputation is then performed using any of the methods we have considered. This allows for variables at any point in time to be used as predictors for variables at any other point in time. Once the data have been imputed, the data set can be reformatted so that there are multiple records for each individual, one record for each point in time.

MI Example 3

Here is an example of multiple imputation of longitudinal data using the simpler method just discussed. The sample consisted of 220 white women, at least 60 years old, who were treated surgically for a hip fracture in the greater Philadelphia area (Mossey, Knott, & Craik, 1990). After their release from the hospital, they were interviewed three times: at 2 months, 6 months, and 12 months. The following five variables, measured at each of the three waves, were considered.

CESD   A measure of depression, on a scale from 0 to 60.
SRH   Self-rated health, measured on a four-point scale (1 = poor, 4 = excellent).

WALK   Coded 1 if the patient could walk without aid at home; otherwise coded 0.

ADL   Number of self-care "activities of daily living" that could be completed without assistance (ranges from 0 to 3).

PAIN   Degree of pain experienced by the patient [ranges from 0 (none) to 6 (constant)].

Our goal was to estimate a "fixed-effects" linear regression model (Greene, 2000) with CESD as the dependent variable and the other four as independent variables. The model has the form

$$y_{it} = \alpha_i + \beta_1 x_{it1} + \cdots + \beta_4 x_{it4} + \varepsilon_{it},$$

where y_{it} is value of CESD for person i at time t and the ε_{it} satisfy the usual assumptions of the linear model. What is noteworthy about this model is that there is a different intercept α_i for each person in the sample, thereby controlling for all stable characteristics of the patients. This person-specific intercept also induces a correlation among the multiple responses for each individual.

To estimate the model, a working data set of 660 observations, one for each person at each point in time, was created. There are two equivalent computational methods for getting the OLS regression estimates: (1) include a dummy variable for each person (less 1) or (2) run the regression on deviation scores. This second method involves subtracting the person-specific mean (over the three time points) from each variable in the model before running the multiple regression.

Unfortunately, there was a substantial amount of attrition from the study, along with additional nonresponse at each of the time points. If we delete all person-times with any missing data, the working data set is reduced from 660 observations to 453 observations. If we delete all *persons* with missing data on any variable at any time, the data set is reduced to 101 persons (or 303 person-times).

Table 6.4 displays fixed-effects regression results using four methods for handling the missing data.[15] The first two columns give coefficients and standard errors for two versions of listwise deletion: (1) deletion of persons with any missing data and (2) deletion of person-times with any missing data. There is clear evidence that the level of depression is affected by self-rated health, but only marginal evidence for an effect of walking ability. It is also evident that the level of depression in waves 1 and 2 was much higher than in wave 3 (when most of the

TABLE 6.4

Coefficient Estimates (and Standard Errors)
for Fixed-Effects Models Predicting CESD

	Listwise Deletion by Person	Listwise Deletion by Person-Time	Data Augmentation by Person-Time	Data Augmentation by Person
SRH	2.341 (0.586)**	1.641 (0.556)**	2.522 (0.617)**	1.538 (0.501)**
WALK	−1.552 (0.771)*	−1.381 (0.761)	−1.842 (0.960)	−0.550 (0.825)
ADL	−0.676 (0.528)	−0.335 (0.539)	−0.385 (0.562)	−0.410 (0.435)
PAIN	0.031 (0.179)	0.215 (0.168)	0.305 (0.180)	0.170 (0.164)
WAVE 1	8.004 (0.650)**	8.787 (0.613)**	6.900 (0.729)**	9.112 (0.615)**
WAVE 2	7.045 (0.579)**	7.930 (0.520)**	5.808 (0.642)**	8.131 (0.549)**
N (person-times)	303	453	660	660

*$p < .05$, **$p < .01$.

patients had fully recovered). There is little or no evidence for effects of ADL and PAIN.

The last two columns give results based on the full sample, with missing data imputed by data augmentation under the multivariate normal model.[16] For results in the third column, the imputation was carried out on the 660 person-times treated as independent observations. Thus, missing data were imputed using only information at the same point in time. To do the imputation for the last column, the data were reorganized into 220 persons with distinct variable names for each time point. In this way, each variable with missing data was imputed based on information at all three points in time. In principle, this should produce much better imputations, especially because a missing value could be predicted by measurements of the same variable at different points in time.

In fact, the estimated standard errors for the last column are all a bit lower than those for the penultimate column. They also tend to be a bit lower than those for either of the two listwise deletion methods. On the other hand, the standard errors for data augmentation based on person-times tend to be somewhat larger than those for the two listwise deletion methods. In any case, there is no overwhelming advantage to multiple imputation in this application. Qualitatively, the conclusions would be pretty much the same regardless of the imputation method.

7. NONIGNORABLE MISSING DATA

Previous chapters have focused on methods for situations in which the missing data mechanism is ignorable. Ignorability implies that we do not have to model the process by which data happen to be missing. The key requirement for ignorability is that the data are missing at random—the probability of missing data on a particular variable does not depend on the values of that variable (net of other variables in the analysis).

The basic strategy for dealing with ignorable missing data is easily summarized: Adjust for all observable differences between missing and nonmissing cases, and assume that all remaining differences are unsystematic. This is, of course, a familiar strategy. Standard regression models are designed to do just that—adjust for observed differences and assume that unobserved differences are unsystematic.

Unfortunately, there are often strong reasons to suspect that data are *not* missing at random. Common sense tells us, for example, that people who have been arrested are less likely to report their arrest status than people who have not been arrested. People with high incomes may be less likely to report their incomes. In clinical drug trials, people who are getting worse are more likely to drop out than people who are getting better.

What should be done in these situations? There *are* models and methods for handling nonignorable missing data, and it is natural to want to apply them. However, it is no accident that there is little software available for estimating nonignorable models (with one important exception—Heckman's selectivity bias model). The basic problem is that, given a model for the data, there is only one ignorable missing data mechanism, but there are infinitely many different nonignorable missing data mechanisms. So it is hard to write computer programs that will handle even a fraction of the possibilities. Furthermore, the answers may vary widely depending on the model chosen. So it is critically important to choose the right model, and that choice requires very accurate and detailed knowledge of the phenomenon under investigation. Worse still, there is no empirical way to discriminate one nonignorable model from another (or from the ignorable model).

I will not go so far as to say, "Don't go there," but I will say this: "If you choose to go there, do so with extreme caution." In addition, if you do not have much statistical expertise, make sure you find a collaborator who does. Keeping these caveats in mind, this chapter is designed to give you a brief introduction and overview to some approaches for dealing with nonignorable missing data.

The first thing you need to know is that the two methods I have been pushing for *ignorable* missing data—maximum likelihood and multiple imputation—can be readily adapted to deal with nonignorable missing data. If the chosen model is correct (a big if), these two methods have the same optimal properties that they have in the ignorable setting. A second point to remember is that any method for nonignorable missing data should be accompanied by a sensitivity analysis. Because results can vary widely depending on the assumed model, it is important to try out a range of plausible models and see if they give similar answers.

Two Classes of Models

Regardless of whether you choose maximum likelihood or multiple imputation, there are two quite different approaches to modeling non-ignorable missing data: selection models and pattern-mixture models. This is most easily explained for a single variable with missing data. Let Y be the variable of interest and let R be a dummy variable with a value of 1 if Y is observed and 0 if Y is missing. Let $f(Y, R)$ be the joint probability density function (p.d.f.) for the two variables. Choosing a model means choosing some explicit specification for $f(Y, R)$.

The joint p.d.f. can be factored in two different ways (Little and Rubin, 1987). In selection models we use

$$f(Y, R) = \Pr(R|Y)f(Y),$$

where $f(Y)$ is the marginal density of Y and $\Pr(R|Y)$ is the conditional probability of R given some value of Y. In words, we first model Y as if no data were missing. Then, given a value of Y, we model whether or not the data are missing. For example, we could assume that $f(Y)$ is a normal distribution with mean μ and variance σ^2, and that $\Pr(R|Y)$ is given by

$$\Pr(R = 1|Y) = \begin{cases} p_1 & \text{if } Y > 0, \\ p_2 & \text{if } Y \leq 0. \end{cases}$$

This model is identified and can be estimated by ML.

The alternative factorization of the joint p.d.f. corresponds to pattern-mixture models,

$$f(Y, R) = f(Y|R) \Pr(R),$$

where $f(Y|R)$ is the density for Y conditional on whether Y is missing or not. For example, we could presume that $\Pr(R)$ is just some constant θ and $f(Y|R)$ is a normal distribution with variance σ^2 and mean μ_1 if $R = 1$ and mean μ_0 if $R = 0$. Unfortunately, this model is not identified and, hence, cannot be estimated without further restrictions on the parameters.

Pattern-mixture models may seem like an unnatural way to think about the missing data mechanism. Typically, we suppose that the values of the data (in this case Y) are predetermined. Then, depending on the data collection procedure, the values of Y may have some impact on whether or not we actually obtain the desired information. This way of thinking corresponds to selection models. Pattern-mixture models, on the other hand, seem to reverse the direction of causality, allowing missingness to affect the distribution of the variable of interest. Of course, conditional probability is agnostic with respect to the direction of causality, and it turns out that pattern-mixture models are sometimes easier to work with than the more theoretically appealing selection models, especially for multiple imputation. I now consider some examples of both selection models and pattern-mixture models.

Heckman's Model for Sample Selection Bias

Heckman's (1976) model for sample selection bias is the classic example of a selection model for missing data. The model is designed for situations in which the dependent variable in a linear regression model is missing for some cases, but not for others. A common motivating example is a regression that predicts women's wages, where wage data are necessarily missing for women who are not in the labor force. It is natural to suppose that women are less likely to enter the labor force if their wages would be low. Hence, the data are not missing at random.

Heckman formulated his model in terms of latent variables, but I will work with a more direct specification. For a sample of n cases

$(i = 1, \ldots, n)$, let Y_i be a normally distributed variable with a variance σ^2 and a mean given by

$$E(Y_i) = \beta X_i, \qquad [7.1]$$

where X_i is a column vector of independent variables (including a value of 1 for the intercept) and β is a row vector of coefficients. The goal is to estimate β. If all Y_i were observed, we could get ML estimates of β by ordinary least squares regression. However, some Y_i are missing. The probability of missing data on Y_i is assumed to follow a probit model,

$$\Pr(R_i = 0 | Y_i, X_i) = \Phi(\alpha_0 + \alpha_1 Y_i + \alpha_2 X_i), \qquad [7.2]$$

where $\Phi(\cdot)$ is the cumulative distribution function for a standard normal variable. Unless $\alpha_1 = 0$, the data are *not* missing at random because the probability of missingness depends on Y.

This model is identified (even when there are no X_i or when X_i does not enter the probit equation) and can be estimated by maximum likelihood. The likelihood for an observation with Y observed is

$$\Pr(R_i = 1 | y_i, x_i) f(y_i | x_i)$$
$$= [1 - \Phi(\alpha_0 + \alpha_1 y_i + \alpha_2 x_i)] \phi\left(\frac{y_i - \beta x_i}{\sigma}\right) \sigma^{-1}, \qquad [7.3]$$

where $\phi(\cdot)$ is the density function for a standard normal variable. For an observation with Y missing, the likelihood is

$$\int_{-\infty}^{+\infty} \Pr(R_i = 0 | y, x_i) f(y | x_i) \, dy = \Phi\left(\frac{\alpha_0 + (\alpha_1 \beta + \alpha_2) x_i}{\sqrt{1 + \alpha_1^2 \sigma^2}}\right). \qquad [7.4]$$

Equation 7.4 follows from the general principle that the likelihood for an observation with missing data can be found by integrating the likelihood over all possible values of the missing data. The likelihood for the entire sample can be readily maximized using standard numerical methods.

Unfortunately, estimates produced by this method are extremely sensitive to the assumption that Y has a normal distribution. If Y actually has a skewed distribution, ML estimates obtained under

Heckman's model may be severely biased, perhaps even more than estimates obtained under an ignorable missing data model (Little & Rubin, 1987).

Heckman also proposed a two-step estimator that is less sensitive to departures from normality, substantially easier to compute and, therefore, more popular than ML. However, the two-step method has its own limitations.

In brief, the two steps are as follows:

1. Estimate a probit regression of R—the missing data indicator—on the X variables.
2. For cases that have data present on Y, estimate a least-squares linear regression of Y on X plus a variable that is a transformation of the predicted values from the probit regression.[17]

Unlike the ML method, the two-step procedure is not feasible if there are no X variables. Furthermore, the parameters are only weakly identified if the X variables are the same in the probit and linear regressions. To get reasonably stable estimates, it is essential that there be X variables in the probit regression that are excluded from the linear regression. Of course, it is rare that such exclusion restrictions can be persuasively justified. Even when all these conditions are met, the two-step estimator may perform poorly in many realistic situations (Stolzenberg & Relles, 1990, 1997).

Given the apparent sensitivity of these sample selection methods to violations of assumptions, how should we proceed to do a sensitivity analysis? For the ML estimator, the key assumption is the normality of the dependent variable Y. So a natural strategy would be to fit models that assume different distributions. Skewed distributions like Weibull or gamma probably would be most useful because it is the symmetry of the normal distribution that is most crucial for ML. ML estimation should be possible for alternative distributions, although the integral in Equation 7.4 may not have a convenient form and may require numerical integration. For the two-step estimator, the key assumption is the exclusion of certain X variables from the linear regression that predicts Y. A sensitivity analysis might explore the consequences of choosing different sets of X variables for the two equations.

ML Estimation With Pattern-Mixture Models

Pattern-mixture models are notoriously underidentified. Suppose we have two variables X and Y, with four observed patterns of missingness:

1. Both X and Y observed.
2. X observed, Y missing.
3. Y observed, X missing.
4. Both X and Y missing.

Let $R = 1, 2, 3$, or 4, depending on which of these patterns is observed. A pattern-mixture model for these data has the general form

$$f(X, Y, R) = f(Y, X|R)\Pr(R).$$

To make the model more specific, we might suppose that $\Pr(R)$ is given by the set of values p_1, p_2, p_3, and p_4. Then we might assume that $f(Y, X|R)$ is a bivariate normal distribution with the usual parameters: $\mu_X, \mu_Y, \sigma_X, \sigma_Y, \sigma_{XY}$. However, we allow each of these parameters to be different for each value of R. The problem is that when X is observed but Y is not, there is no information to estimate the mean and standard deviation of Y or the covariance of X and Y. Similarly, when Y is observed but X is not, there is no information to estimate the mean and standard deviation of X or the covariance of X and Y. If both variables are missing, we have no information at all.

To make any headway, we must impose some restrictions on the four sets of parameters. Let $\theta^{(i)}$ be the set of parameters for pattern i. A simple but very restrictive condition is to assume that $\theta^{(1)} = \theta^{(2)} = \theta^{(3)} = \theta^{(4)}$, which is equivalent to MCAR. In that case, ML estimation of the pattern-mixture model is identical to that discussed in Chapter 3 for the normal model with ignorable missing data. Little (1993, 1994) proposed other classes of restrictions that do *not* correspond to ignorable missing data, but yield identified models. Here is one example. Let $\theta^{(i)}_{Y|X}$ represent the conditional distribution of Y given X for pattern i. What Little calls complete-case missing-variable restrictions are given by

$$\theta^{(2)}_{Y|X} = \theta^{(1)}_{Y|X},$$
$$\theta^{(3)}_{X|Y} = \theta^{(1)}_{X|Y},$$
$$\theta^{(4)} = \theta^{(1)}.$$

For the two patterns with one variable missing, the conditional distribution of the missing variable given the observed variable is equated to the corresponding distribution for the complete-case pattern. For the pattern with both variables missing, all parameters are assumed equal to those in the complete-case pattern. This model is identified and the ML estimates can be found by noniterative means. Once all these estimates are obtained, they can be easily combined to get estimates of the marginal distribution of X and Y.

Multiple Imputation With Pattern-Mixture Models

ML estimation of pattern mixture models is still rather esoteric at this point in time. Much more practical and useful is the combination of pattern-mixture models with multiple imputation (Rubin, 1987). The simplest strategy is to generate imputations under an ignorable model first and then modify the imputed values using, say, a linear transformation. A sensitivity analysis is then easily obtained by repeating the process with different constants in the linear transformation.

Here is a simple example. Suppose that we again have two variables X and Y, but only two missing data patterns: (1) complete case and (2) missing Y. We assume that within each pattern, X and Y have a bivariate normal distribution. We also believe that cases with missing Y tend to be those with higher values of Y, so we assume that all parameters for the two patterns are the same except that $\mu_Y^{(2)} = c\mu_Y^{(1)}$, where c is some constant greater than 1. Multiple imputation then amounts to generating imputed values for Y under an ignorable missing data mechanism and then multiplying all the imputed values by c. Of course, to make this work, we have choose a value for c, and that choice may be rather arbitrary. A sensitivity analysis consists of reimputing the data and reestimating the model for several different values of c.[18]

Now let us turn this into a real example. For the college data, there were 98 colleges with missing data on the dependent variable GRADRAT. It is plausible to suppose that those colleges that did not report graduation rates had lower graduation rates than those that did report their rates. This speculation is supported by the fact that the mean of the imputed graduation rates for the multiply imputed data described in Chapter 5 is about 10 percentage points lower than the mean graduation rate for the colleges without missing data. However,

TABLE 7.1
Regression of Graduation Rates on Several Variables,
Under Different Pattern-Mixture Models

Variable	100%	90%	80%	70%	60%
CSAT	0.067	0.069	0.071	0.072	0.071
LENROLL	2.039	2.062	2.077	2.398	2.641
PRIVATE	12.716	12.542	11.908	12.675	12.522
STUFAC	−0.217	−0.142	−0.116	−0.126	−0.213
RMBRD	2.383	2.264	2.738	2.513	2.464

this difference is entirely due to differences on the predictor variables and does not constitute evidence that the data are not missing at random.

Suppose, however, that the difference in graduation rates between missing and nonmissing cases is even greater. Specifically, modify the imputed graduation rates so that they are a specified percentage of what would otherwise be imputed under the ignorability assumption. Table 7.1 displays results for imputations that are 100%, 90%, 80%, 70%, and 60% of the original values. For each regression, entirely new imputations were generated. Thus, some of the variation across columns is due to the randomness of the imputation process. In general, the coefficients are quite stable, suggesting that departures from ignorability would not have much impact on the conclusions. The STUFAC coefficient varies the most, but it is far from statistically significant in all cases.

8. SUMMARY AND CONCLUSION

Among conventional methods for handling missing data, listwise deletion is the least problematic. Although listwise deletion may discard a substantial fraction of the data, there is no reason to expect bias unless the data are not missing completely at random. In addition, the standard errors also should be decent estimates of the true standard errors. Furthermore, if you are estimating a linear regression model, listwise deletion is quite robust to situations where there are missing data on an independent variable and the probability of missingness depends on the value of that variable. If you are estimating a logistic regression model, listwise deletion can tolerate either nonrandom missingness on the dependent variable or nonrandom missingness on the independent variables (but not both).

By contrast, all other conventional methods for handling missing data introduce bias into the standard error estimates, and many conventional methods (like dummy variable adjustment) produce biased parameter estimates, even when the data are missing completely at random. So listwise deletion is generally a safer approach.

If the amount of data that must be discarded under listwise deletion is intolerable, then two alternatives to consider are maximum likelihood and multiple imputation. In their standard incarnations, these two methods assume that the data are missing at random, an appreciably weaker assumption than missing completely at random. Under fairly general conditions, these methods produce estimates that are approximately unbiased and efficient. They also produce good estimates of standard errors and test statistics. The downside is that they are more difficult to implement than most conventional methods and multiple imputation gives you slightly different results every time you do it.

If the goal is to estimate a linear model that falls within the class of models estimated by LISREL and similar packages, then maximum likelihood is probably the preferred method. Currently there are at least four statistical packages that can accomplish this, the best known of which is Amos.

If you want to estimate any kind of nonlinear model, then multiple imputation is the way to go. There are many different ways to do multiple imputation. The most widely used method assumes that the variables in the intended model have a multivariate normal distribution. Imputation is accomplished by a Bayesian technique that involves iterated regression imputation with random draws for both the data values and the parameters. Several software packages are currently available to accomplish this.

Other multiple imputation methods that make less restrictive distributional assumptions are currently under development, but they have not yet reached a level of theoretical or computational refinement that would justify widespread use.

It is also possible to do maximum likelihood or multiple imputation under assumptions that the data are not missing at random, but getting good results is tricky. These methods are very sensitive to assumptions made about the missingness mechanism or about the distributions of the variables with missing data. In addition, there is no way to test these assumptions. Hence, the most important requirement is good a priori knowledge of the mechanism for generating the missing data. Any effort to estimate nonignorable models should be accompanied by a sensitivity analysis.

NOTES

1. The proof is straightforward. We want to estimate $f(Y|X)$, the conditional distribution of Y given X, a vector of predictor variables. Let $A = 1$ if all variables are observed; otherwise, $A = 0$. Listwise deletion is equivalent to estimating $f(Y|X, A = 1)$. The aim is to show that this function is the same as $f(Y|X)$. From the definition of conditional probability, we have

$$f(Y|X, A = 1) = \frac{f(Y, X, A = 1)}{f(X, A = 1)}$$

$$= \frac{\Pr(A = 1|Y, X)f(Y|X)f(X)}{\Pr(A = 1|X)f(X)}.$$

Assume that $\Pr(A = 1|Y, X) = \Pr(A = 1|X)$, that is, that the probability of data present on all variables does *not* depend on Y, but may depend on any variables in X. It immediately follows that

$$f(Y|X, A = 1) = f(Y|X).$$

Note that this result applies to any regression procedure, not just linear regression.

2. Even if the probability of missing data depends on both X and Y, there are some situations when listwise deletion is unproblematic. Let $p(Y, X)$ be the probability of missing data on one or more of the variables in the regression model, as a function of the dichotomous dependent variable Y and a vector of independent variables X. If that probability can be factored as $p(Y, X) = f(Y)g(Y)$, then logistic regression slopes using listwise deletion are consistent estimates of the true coefficients (Glynn, 1985).

3. Glasser (1964) derived formulas that are reasonably easy to implement, but valid only when the independent variables and missing data pattern are "fixed" from sample to sample, an unlikely condition for realistic applications. The formulas of Van Praag, Dijkstra, and Van Velzen (1985) are more generally applicable, but require information beyond that given in the covariance matrix: higher-order moments and the number of available cases for all sets of four variables.

4. Although the dummy variable adjustment method is clearly unacceptable when data are truly missing, it may still be appropriate in cases where the unobserved value simply does not exist. For example, married respondents may be asked to rate the quality of their marriage, but that question has no meaning for unmarried respondents. Suppose we assume that there is one linear equation for married couples and another equation for unmarried couples. The married equation is identical to the unmarried equation except that it has (a) a term that corresponds to the effect of marital quality on the dependent variable and (b) a different intercept. It is easy to show that the dummy variable adjustment method produces optimal estimates in this situation.

5. Schafer and Schenker (2000) proposed a method for getting consistent estimates of the standard errors when conditional mean imputation is used. They claim that under appropriate conditions their method can yield more precise estimates with less computational effort than multiple imputation.

6. Maximum likelihood under the multivariate normal assumption produces consistent estimates of the means and the covariance matrix for any multivariate distribution with finite fourth moments (Little & Smith, 1987).

7. This varilable is the sum of two variables in the original data set, "room costs" and "board variable."

8. For the two-step method, it is also possible to get standard error estimates using "sandwich" formulas described by Browne and Arminger (1995).

9. The standard errors were estimated under the assumption of bivariate normality, which is appropriate for this example because the data were drawn from a bivariate normal distribution. The formula is

$$\text{S.E.}(r) = \frac{1 - r^2}{\sqrt{n}}.$$

Although the sample correlation coefficient is not normally distributed, the large sample size in this case should ensure a close approximation to normality. Thus, these standard errors could be appropriately used to construct confidence intervals.

10. For data augmentation, the standard noninformative prior (Schafer, 1997), known as the Jeffreys prior, is written as $|\Sigma|^{-(p+1)/2}$, where Σ is the covariance matrix and p is the number of variables.

11. One way to get such an overdispersed distribution is to use a bootstrap method. For example, take five different random samples, with replacement from the original data set, and compute the EM estimate in each of these samples. The EM estimates then could be used as starting values in each of five parallel chains.

12. An easy way to do this is to divide the (0, 1) interval into five subintervals with lengths proportional to the probabilities for each category of marital status. Draw a random number from a uniform distribution on the unit interval. Assign the marital status category that corresponds to the subinterval in which the random number falls.

13. Actually, the degrees of freedom is equal to the rank of $\mathbf{L}$, which is usually, but not always, r.

14. The nine regions were classified as follows: East (New England, Middle Atlantic), 566 cases; Central (East North Central, West North Central), 715 cases; South (South Atlantic, East South Central, West South Central), 1,095 cases; West (Mountain, Pacific), 616 cases.

15. The regression analysis was performed with the GLM procedure in SAS using the ABSORB statement to handle the fixed effects.

16. Ten data sets were produced, with 30 iterations per data set. After imputation, the imputed values were recoded wherever necessary to preserve the permissible values of the original variables.

17. Specifically, the additional variable is $\lambda(ax_i)$, where a is the row vector of estimated coefficients from the probit model. The function $\lambda(z)$, the inverse Mills function, is defined as $\phi(z)/\Phi(z)$, where $\phi(z)$ is the density function and $\Phi(z)$ is the cumulative distribution function, both for a standard normal variable.

18. In the models considered by Rubin (1987), the conditional prior distribution of the parameters is specified for the missing data pattern given the parameters in the complete data pattern. In the example given here, I have merely assumed that the conditional mean for the missing cases is some multiple of the mean for the complete cases. Additionally, the conditional variance for the missing cases can be allowed to be larger than that for the complete cases to compensate for greater uncertainty.

REFERENCES

AGRESTI, A., and FINLAY, B. (1997). *Statistical methods for the social sciences*. Englewood Cliffs, NJ: Prentice–Hall.

ALLISON, P. D. (1987). Estimation of linear models with incomplete data. In C. Clogg (Ed.), *Sociological methodology 1987* (pp. 71–103). Washington, DC: American Sociological Association.

ALLISON, P. D. (2000). Multiple imputation for missing data. *Sociological Methods & Research, 28*, 301–309.

BARNARD, J., and RUBIN, D. R. (1999). Small-sample degrees of freedom with multiple imputation. *Biometrika, 86*, 948–955.

BEALE, E. M. L., and LITTLE, R. J. A. (1975). Missing values in multivariate analysis. *Journal of the Royal Statistical Society, Series B, 37*, 129–145.

BRAND, J. P. L. (1999). *Development, implementation and evaluation of multiple imputation strategies for the statistical analysis of incomplete data sets*. Ph.D. Thesis, Erasmus University Rotterdam (ISBN 90-74479-08-1).

BROWNE, M. W., and ARMINGER, G. (1995). Specification and estimation of mean and covariance structure models. In G. Arminger, C. C. Clogg, and M. E. Sobel (Eds.), *Handbook of statistical modeling for the social and behavioral sciences* (pp. 185–249). New York: Plenum.

COHEN, J., and COHEN, P. (1985). *Applied multiple regression and correlation analysis for the behavioral sciences* (2nd ed.). Hillsdale, NJ: Erlbaum.

DAVIS, J. A., and SMITH, T. W. (1997). *General social surveys, 1972–1996*. Chicago, IL: National Opinion Research Center (producer); Ann Arbor, MI: Interuniversity Consortium for Political and Social Research (distributor).

DEMPSTER, A. P., LAIRD, N. M., and RUBIN, D. B. (1977). Maximum likelihood estimation from incomplete data via the EM algorithm. *Journal of the Royal Statistical Society, Series B, 39*, 1–38.

FUCHS, C. (1982). Maximum likelihood estimation and model selection in contingency tables with missing data. *Journal of the American Statistical Association, 77*, 270–278.

GLASSER, M. (1964). Linear regression analysis with missing observations among the independent variables. *Journal of the American Statistical Association, 59*, 834–844.

GLYNN, R. (1985). *Regression estimates when nonresponse depends on the outcome variable*. Unpublished doctoral dissertation, School of Public Health, Harvard University.

GOURIEROUX, C., and MONFORT, A. (1981). On the problem of missing data in linear models. *Review of Economic Studies, 48*, 579–586.

GREENE, W. H. (2000). *Econometric analysis* (4th ed.). Englewood Cliffs, NJ: Prentice–Hall.

HAITOVSKY, Y. (1968). Missing data in regression analysis. *Journal of the Royal Statistical Society, Series B, 30*, 67–82.

HECKMAN, J. J. (1976). The common structure of statistical models of truncated, sample selection and limited dependent variables, and a simple estimator of such models. *Annals of Economic and Social Measurement, 5*, 475–492.

90

IVERSEN, G. (1985). *Bayesian statistical inference*. Sage University Papers Series on Quantitative Applications in Social Science, 07-43. Thousand Oaks, CA: Sage.

JONES, M. P. (1996). Indicator and stratification methods for missing explanatory variables in multiple linear regression. *Journal of the American Statistical Association, 91*, 222–230.

KIM, J.-O., and CURRY, J. (1977). The treatment of missing data in multivariate analysis. *Sociological Methods & Research, 6*, 215–240.

KING, G., HONAKER, J., JOSEPH, A., SCHEVE, K., and SINGH, N. (1999). *AMELIA: A program for missing data*. Unpublished program manual. Available at http://gking.harvard.edu/stats.shtml.

KING, G., HONAKER, J., JOSEPH, A., and SCHEVE, K. (2001). Analyzing incomplete political science data: An alternative algorithm for multiple imputation. *American Political Science Review, 95*, 49–69. Available at http://gking.harvard.edu/stats.shtml.

LANDERMAN, L. R., LAND, K. C., and PIEPER, C. F. (1997). An empirical evaluation of the predictive mean matching method for imputing missing values. *Sociological Methods & Research, 26*, 3–33.

LI, K. H., MENG, X. L., RAGHUNATHAN, T. E., and RUBIN, D. B. (1991). Significance levels from repeated p-values and multiply imputed data. *Statistica Sinica, 1*, 65–92.

LITTLE, R. J. A. (1988). Missing data in large surveys (with discussion). *Journal of Business and Economic Statistics, 6*, 287–301.

LITTLE, R. J. A. (1992). Regression with missing X's: A review. *Journal of the American Statistical Association, 87*, 1227–1237.

LITTLE, R. J. A. (1993). Pattern-mixture models for multivariate incomplete data. *Journal of the American Statistical Association, 88*, 125–134.

LITTLE, R. J. A. (1994). A class of pattern-mixture models for normal incomplete data. *Biometrika, 81*, 471–483.

LITTLE, R. J. A., and RUBIN, D. B. (1987). *Statistical analysis with missing data*. New York: Wiley.

LITTLE, R. J. A., and SMITH, P. J. (1987). Editing and imputation for quantitative survey data. *Journal of the American Statistical Association, 82*, 58–68.

MARINI, M. M., OLSEN, A. R., and RUBIN, D. (1979). Maximum likelihood estimation in panel studies with missing data. In K. F. Schuessler (Ed.), *Sociological methodology 1980* (pp. 314–357). San Francisco: Jossey-Bass.

McCULLAGH, P. (1980). Regression models for ordinal data (with discussion). *Journal of the Royal Statistical Society, Series B, 42*, 109–142.

McLACHLAN, G. J., and KRISHNAN, T. (1997). *The EM algorithm and extensions*. New York: Wiley.

MOSSEY, J. M., KNOTT, K., and CRAIK, R. (1990). Effects of persistent depressive symptoms on hip fracture recovery. *Journal of Gerontology: Medical Sciences, 45*, M163–168.

MUTHÉN, B., KAPLAN, K., and HOLLIS, M. (1987). On structural equation modeling with data that are not missing completely at random. *Psychometrika, 42*, 431–462.

RAGHUNATHAN, T. E., LEPKOWSKI, J. M., VAN HOEWYK, J., and SOLENBERGER, P. (1999). *A multivariate technique for multiply imputing missing values using a sequence of regression models*. Unpublished manuscript. Contact teraghu@umich.edu.

ROBINS, J. M., and WANG, N. (2000). Inference for imputation estimators. *Biometrika*, 87, 113–124.

RUBIN, D. B. (1976). Inference and missing data. *Biometrika*, 63, 581–592.

RUBIN, D. B. (1987). *Multiple Imputation for Nonresponse in Surveys*. New York: Wiley.

RUBIN, D. B., and SCHENKER, N. (1991). Multiple imputation in health-care databases: An overview and some applications. *Statistics in Medicine*, 10, 585–598.

SCHAFER, J. L. (1997). *Analysis of Incomplete Multivariate Data*. London: Chapman & Hall.

SCHAFER, J. L., and SCHENKER, N. (2000). Inference with imputed conditional means. *Journal of the American Statistical Association*, 95, 144–154.

SCHENKER, N., and TAYLOR, J. M. G. (1996). Partially parametric techniques for multiple imputation. *Computational Statistics and Data Analysis*, 22, 425–446.

STOLZENBERG, R. M., and RELLES, D. A. (1990). Theory testing in a world of constrained research design: The significance of Heckman's censored sampling bias correction for nonexperimental research. *Sociological Methods & Research*, 18, 395–415.

STOLZENBERG, R. M., and RELLES, D. A. (1997). Tools for intuition about sample selection bias and its correction. *American Sociological Review*, 62, 494–507.

VACH, W. (1994). *Logistic Regression with Missing Values in the Covariates*. New York: Springer-Verlag.

VACH, W., and BLETTNER, M. (1991). Biased estimation of the odds ratio in case-control studies due to the use of ad hoc methods of correcting for missing values for confounding variables. *American Journal of Epidemiology*, 134, 895–907.

VAN BUUREN, S., and OUDSHOORN, K. (1999). Flexible multiple imputation by MICE. Report TNO-PG 99.054, TNO Prevention and Health, Leiden. Available at http://www.multiple-imputation.com/

VAN PRAAG, B. M. S., DIJKSTRA, T. K., and VAN VELZEN, J. (1985). Least-squares theory based on general distributional assumptions with an application to the incomplete observations problem. *Psychometrika*, 50, 25–36.

WANG, N., and ROBINS, J. M. (1998). Large sample inference in parametric multiple imputation. *Biometrika*, 85, 935–948.

WINSHIP, C., and RADBILL, L. (1994). Sampling weights and regression analysis. *Sociological Methods & Research*, 23, 230–257.

ABOUT THE AUTHOR

PAUL D. ALLISON is Professor of Sociology at the University of Pennsylvania. He received his Ph.D. in sociology from the University of Wisconsin in 1976, and did postdoctoral study in statistics at the University of Chicago and the University of Pennsylvania. He has published 5 books and more than 25 articles on statistical methods in the social sciences. These publications have dealt with a wide variety of methods, including linear regression, log-linear analysis, logit analysis, probit analysis, measurement error, inequality measures, missing data, Markov processes, and event history analysis. Recent books include *Multiple Regression: A Primer* and *Logistic Regression Using the SAS System: Theory and Application*. He is currently writing a book on fixed-effects methods for the analysis of longitudinal data. Each summer he teaches five-day workshops on event history analysis and categorical data analysis that draw nearly 100 researchers from around the United States. His substantive interests include scientists' careers and theories of altruistic behavior.